Greg

The Spiritual Adventures

of an Ordinary Girl/Psychic Medium

by

Keely Potts

Dedication

This book is dedicated to my beautiful little boy, Loxley. You make my heart complete. You are my world, and Everything I do, I do it for you. ♡

Acknowledgements

Firstly, I'd like to say a massive thank you to Michelle Emerson. Without your guidance and support this book wouldn't have been possible. Thank you for spurring me on every step along the way and giving me a push when I felt like giving up! I've really enjoyed our chatterbox moments, usually containing at least a half an hour discussion on George Michael, and fantastic cups of tea made by the wonderful Hannah. Thank you. ♡

Throughout my 32 years on this Earth plane I really have met some wonderful people. I was very blessed to be born to such lovely parents, Anthony & Karen. They not only gave me life but they have supported me through thick and thin. In my crazy childhood years, when I was opening up to the world of spirit, they never once lost patience with me. Thank you for everything that you have done for me. I love you both so much. ♡ xxx

To my sister, Emily. You may not have been my first choice in sisters (I wanted a blonde-haired sister, not a chimpanzee, but hey ho, Grandad Hopper said, 'you get what you are given' so I'll go with that one) but you are a good one! Thank you for all of our bonkers memories! I love you and I'm so proud of the beautiful, intelligent and brave woo-man you have become. ♡ xxx

To the other half of me, My Matthew. I don't think I could ever in a million years find anyone else that just 'gets me' the way that you do. We have been through so much together, but what I love about you is your strength! Even after everything, we still laugh and joke around like we are the children we were when we first met. You are my soul mate and I absolutely adore you! I'm looking forward to the next chapter in our lives and seeing what wonderful adventures we can get up to! ♡ xxx

A very special mention to my Aunty Pamela, the only lady who has ever fully understood my spiritual gift. I've always felt like I've been able to talk to you about it all, even the most random of stuff that spirit have given me, you've always given me the confidence to say it. I love you to the moon and stars and back again. ♡ xxx

To one of the bravest ladies I've ever met, my Aunty Alison. You are such an amazing woman, you have been through so much yet you are always there to help and support everyone around you. You are also the next up and coming psychic medium!! Can't ever pull the wool over your eyes! Love you. ♡

To my baby lady & cousin, Megan. You are the funniest, cleverest, beautifulest, young and caring girl I've ever known! It's a laugh a minute when you are around! It's been such a privilege to watch you grow up into the gorgeous girl you have become. Your dad would be so proud of you, and he would be of Lewis too ♥ love you all of the world xxx

A special shout out to my scotty girls. Sara & my lovely god-daughter Skye~Lucia, the best tag team I've ever known. Life has been tough for you both, but I promise you that good things are coming your way! You are both loved and I will always be here for you. ♥ xxx

I'd also like to say a massive thank you to my potsie sisters! A special shout out to Elizabeth, Nina, Helen, Jenny, and Alieshia! Thank you for all of our long chats, and for all of your guidance whilst going through the hell of POTS. You are all amazing and I'm so proud to call you my friends~potsie sisters for life ♥xxx

A very special thank you to everyone that I haven't already mentioned, who have been a part of my journey. My family, my friends, and all of my clients, far and wide. You all make my life complete. ♥xxx

And lastly, a special thought to those that are forever in my heart, my beautiful babies who sadly didn't make it to me in this lifetime... you are loved and thought about each and every day. ♥ My heart will always ache for you xxx

Contents

Why You Need to Buy This Book

✓ Are you slightly sceptical about life after death and would love to read about some real proof?

✓ Are you just a teensy bit nosey and love reading about other people's lives?

✓ Are you a psychic or interested in mediumship and would love to find out how spirit have guided me to where I am today?

Then you're going to LOVE *Greg Said...*

There are plenty of stories about spirit, including:

• the early arrival of Greg – my trusted spirit guide who has been by my side ever since (well, apart from a little gap after he had a run-in with my dad)

• visitations from famous names who have passed over (including one of the most iconic names in pop music)

- hush-hush celebrity readings (where I don't get to find out who I'm reading for until I walk through their hotel room door)

- everyday spirit encounters while I'm out shopping or on holiday (and spirit force me to pass on their messages whether I like it or not)

- and some solid evidence that spirit messages and predictions really can come true.

AND you'll discover more about my life in Bishop Auckland, Co Durham – including my primary school years and the fun I had with Greg, my not-so-fun private education at a local convent school, life with my childhood sweetheart, the chronic illnesses I thought were going to finish me off, and the tragic loss of my three babies.

So grab your copy of this book right now, but be warned... you'll need to clear your diary for a few hours because once you start reading you won't be able to stop!

Introduction

I'm a big believer in synchronicity, and that's why I know you've been drawn to this book for a reason.

The reason may not become clear until you've actually finished reading but please believe me when I tell you that you've found me and *Greg Said* at just the right time in your life.

You may have picked up this book because you're fascinated by all things psychic and spiritual, or you're looking for proof (and perhaps some comfort) that the afterlife exists. And you'll find all of this (and heaps more) as you delve further into the book.

Similarly, you may have stumbled across this book 'by accident' simply because you were searching for a new memoir or autobiography, and if that's the case I really do hope you find it entertaining and that it spurs you into finding out more about spirit.

What this book will most certainly show you is how I manage to combine my two crazy worlds. It can be quite a challenge sometimes (particularly if I'm lying on a sun lounger in Spain and spirit are telling me to pass on a message to the French ladies at the other side of the pool). And at other times, I feel so completely overwhelmed to have been trusted with this special gift, especially when I see the impact it has on people's lives. And whether I'm wearing my white witch/psychic medium hat, or I'm being mam, wife, daughter, sister or friend to my nearest and dearest, I can honestly say that I love every minute of my life.

Perhaps this might be a good time to tell you that this book almost didn't happen...

Over the years, lots of people have said I should write a book. I've thought about it for years, too, but never did anything about it. Then the perfect opportunity appeared this summer. I knew it was the right time. But after writing just the first chapter, I had a wobble and seriously thought about giving it up as a bad idea. Thankfully, I was talked out of it, and here we are, three months later, with the first draft being proofread and edited.

Why am I telling you this? Because I want you to know that if you're reading this and thinking of writing a book, but you keep coming up with excuses as to why you shouldn't, then try to find a way through these wobbles. Writing a book has been an absolute ball for me, and I'm sure that if you could just make a start on yours, you too would enjoy the book creation ride.

Being Psychic

I was an Indigo child, which means I've been able to see and hear spirit from as far back as I can remember. Indigo children are often seen as intuitive, strong-willed, empathetic, and inquisitive: and yes, I showed all those traits. I'm still all of those things today too!

As well as having a supportive and wonderful 'living' family around me, I also love having my Hovis boy, Greg, with me and 'the see-through people' as I used to call them when I was younger.

Why I love my job

The messages I've been able to give people over the years always astounds me. Offering comfort to grieving parents, no matter how small the message, is something very close to my heart.

But what always makes me smile is when I come across a sceptic (my dad was one for years, as you'll find out, until his Tramadol experience) and I can give them a message that shocks them into silence. After that, many become regular clients, and are probably much more open to receiving messages from that point forward.

"Can you just tune into people, Keely?"

This is something I'm asked all the time. The answer is always 'no'. Spirit choose me. And I can't dictate when they can speak to me and when they can't, either. So this often means that when I'm food shopping with my husband, and Greg suddenly appears, I know I will have no choice but to pass on a message to the lady on the till or the man in front of me in the queue. They make the rules, I just have to be the go-between.

My psychic skills have brought me some fab opportunities too...

As well as offering card readings for clients, blessing houses, and helping spirit move from one realm to another, I've also been able to use my gift in other ways. I've featured in *Take a Break's Fame and Fortune* magazine where I've been a 'Psychic Under The Spotlight' (and scored 19 out of 20 for psychic accuracy). I've also read for a few celebrities (you'll find out more about this later - but I'll warn you now that I'm not at liberty to name names).

I've tried to be as open and honest as I can in this book. I've shared some of my darkest times, just so you can see the 'real' Keely, and not just the psychic medium Keely. And I've shared some of the fun, excitement and bonkers stuff too.

I really hope you enjoy reading *Greg Said...* and that it helps you find comfort, inspiration or solace – whatever you're searching for at this point in time.

Chapter 1 ~ Indigo Days and Mama Rosa

"If you enter this world knowing you are loved and you leave this world knowing the same, then everything that happens in between can be dealt with."

~ Michael Jackson

"I've gone, Keely, tell them I've gone."

I will never ever forget those words and that very night back in August 1987. You see, I was only a very young child at the time. I couldn't understand why I was seeing and hearing my great grandmother as she sat there on the end of my bed sinking her small, frail body into my dusky pink bed sheets. I was scared. Although I was only two years old, I remember her like it was yesterday.

I can't remember anything about my life before this moment but the sheer terror I felt that night will always stay with me.

Once again, she whispered to me, "Keely, please tell them I have gone to heaven now." She smiled and in the blink of an eye

1

she had gone. And that was where it all began. Because I was so young I had absolutely no idea how to explain this. Why was Great Gran Smith sat on my bed? What was this place called heaven that she spoke about?

The day after, I remember people in my family talking about these things called funerals?

"Keely, we can't go to see Great Gran Smith today, she died last night." Those were the words that came out of my dad's mouth. Obviously, I really wouldn't have had a clue what he was talking about, but he has since told me that I turned to him and very calmly and clearly said the word 'heaven', and gave him a big wide smile.

My family have always known I was, shall we say, 'different'. Apparently upon my entry into the world I took my time and gobsmacked a few midwives along the way! According to my dad, as soon as my head popped out all he saw were my big blue eyes, wide-open, and starting around the room. Once I'd slowly took in my surroundings I let out the loudest of screams.

"How strange! We've never seen that before," laughed the midwives.

"She has those eyes, Anthony. Psychic blue eyes." That's what my dad's sister, Aunty Pamela, used to say to him! She has always been known to be a bit 'odd' too; very open to the spiritual realm and extremely susceptible to people's energies and feelings. "I'll take her to spiritual church when she is older," she said. And she stuck to her word on that one.

Starting School

Being an August baby meant I was always the youngest in the class (and by far the smallest and daintiest in my first school year).

When I started school, I had only just turned four years-old and I remember feeling as though I were surrounded by giants. Everyone seemed to tower above me. My navy-blue uniform swamped my little frame, but I was ok.

You see, I've always felt ok, strangely safe and comfortable in my own skin, even when I was surrounded by 'giants'. I think it's because I've always known I'm never alone.

One of my earliest memories (apart from Great Gran Smith, of course) comes from those early days at school. It was the end of November, and the teachers had the main doors held open while they carried in Christmas decorations. They asked me to help carry in the tinsel. I will never forget this small little cardboard box that was full of dusty, sparse, scraggy red tinsel.

It was a Friday afternoon and freezing cold as we tottered back and forth from the teacher's car to the hall across the slippery yard. You know that kind of weather where you can see your breath when you talk? It was like that, and it was getting dark.

"It'll soon be home time, Keely," said my lovely teacher, "we'd best get busy." I remember going back in the hall, the teacher closed the doors and the room soon started to warm up. Watery windows, as I call it, started to appear on the window panes. We were asked to take the tinsel out of the boxes so the teachers could put it on to the bushy, spikey, green tree. I was joined by another little boy, he was only small too, but he wasn't in my class, he was older than me. I can't remember his name, but I do remember he had brown hair and big brown eyes.

"You are doing a great job organising that tinsel, boys and girls. This tree is going to look great," smiled the teacher. I was chuffed. The little boy had a knotted piece of purple tinsel and he was flapping it around, trying to untangle it.

"I'll help you," I said. I was always really good at getting knots out of things. "It will snap if you pull it too hard," I said as I reached for the tinsel. As I gently pulled it from his hand the strangest thing happened. I went really, really cold and I felt frightened, just like that night when Great Gran Smith told me she was going to heaven.

"I'm Tommy. Well, my name is Thomas but they used to call me Tommy. Tell the little boy this, Keely. Keely say it, please, please say it. "I'm in heaven now" I'm the little boy's grandad."

"Is your grandad called Tommy?" The words blurted out of my mouth before I could even think about them.

He looked at me with his big brown eyes and his mouth kind of half open. "Yes," he said, "but he went to heaven last week."

"Ok," I said, as I was still trying to untie the piece of tinsel without it breaking. All the while, I could hear this voice chatting in my ear. It was the voice of a young boy.

And Along Came Greg

Standing at my left-hand side was a young boy. He was see-through, and looked to be quite a bit older than me. I remember seeing his big, cheeky grin and lots of freckles. He was wearing brown corduroy knickerbockers with scratchy long socks (he always talks about his scratchy long socks – even now, twenty-odd years later) and scuffed, black lace-up boots. He looked like he had been climbing walls and getting into mischief.

"I'm Greg," he said. "You're the only one who can see me."

I couldn't reply. I didn't know what was happening. I didn't understand what he meant.

Since that day in November 1989, I've been able to see and hear Greg. Some days I can hear him crystal clear, and other days he sounds like a half-tuned radio, crackling away in the distance.

Being four years old and having an imaginary friend is quite the norm, isn't it? That's what my parents thought at first but after years and years of having to buckle Greg in the car, setting an extra place for dinner in case Greg got hungry, and, of course, putting out the sleeping bag and pillow each night because Greg needed sleep too, their patience was tested!! She'll grow out of it, that's what they all would say whenever Greg was mentioned.

Let me tell you a little bit about Greg. He's 12 years-old, and hasn't grown up, but he's very wise for his age. Over the years, he has told me very little about himself, but he's told me all sorts about other people. For years I called him my Hovis boy because that's exactly what he looks like. I remember seeing a TV advert for Hovis bread when I was maybe eight or nine years-old and screaming to my grandmother, "That's what Greg looks like." He even had a bike just like the Hovis bread boy! He has dark hair but always wears a cap, and gorgeous porcelain skin with lots of striking freckles.

Before I move on to tell you about Mama Rosa, my family's restaurant, I have another couple of stories about school, one in particular that's etched on my brain which I think you'll enjoy. Not sure my dad will, though.

When I was at primary school, as daft as this sounds, I always knew what would be for lunch that day. We never had any meal plans, or set days for certain foods. What I did have, though, was my secret weapon – Greg. Each morning when I woke up, I'd hear Greg telling me what was on the lunch menu that day.

"You're getting spaghetti hoops and gravy today!"

I'd think to myself, no, no it won't be that! I'll ask for something different. Lo and behold, however, I'd get to the end of the dinner queue and my tray would be swimming with a lump of mash potato covered in spaghetti hoops and gravy! Yak! Greg – 1, Keely – 0.

As well as keeping me clued up about lunch, Greg would also let me know when one of my classmates was going to be off school. He would point to someone and say, "She won't be at school tomorrow, she's going to have tummy ache."

At first, I didn't tell anyone but it started happening more and more. "Such and such isn't going to be in tomorrow because his nana is going into hospital tonight." I'd go into school the following day and tell my friends why 'such and such' wasn't in the playground. I was always right – or should I say Greg was always right? We knew before the teachers.

One morning on our way to school, I remember telling my dad that I would be staying at Gran Hopper's house in a few days because we were going to have loads of snow and the school heating system would break. Dad did the whole 'eye roll' thing – as he usually does.

"There's no snow forecast, Keely. I think you just want a few days off school, don't you?"

Sure enough, a few days later we had a massive snowfall. I looked out of my bedroom window and could see the cars all snagged up behind each other, and sliding around. I was quite pleased with my little self and couldn't help giving Dad my biggest smile as I ate my breakfast! To prove a point, Dad walked me to school and his face lit up when he saw the gates wide open and other children being dropped off.

"Looks like you were wrong, Keely. School is on," he said with a cheeky glint in his eyes! Maybe Greg had lied to me. Maybe I'd got it wrong this time. I wasn't happy. I didn't like getting things wrong. Off I stomped into school leaving a trail of awful black slush along the floor from my Ladybird welly boots. There weren't many kids at school that day because lots of them lived quite a distance away. I had no excuse, however, because our cottage was only a ten-minute stroll down the road!

Anyway, we all congregated in the school hall and were kept busy with reading and colouring books. I remember getting the crayons out and drawing flowers on a sheet of paper. About half an hour had passed when one of the teachers popped her head around the door.

"We're just trying to contact your parents, girls and boys. The heating has broken so you will all need to go home!"

I was so happy I began jumping up and down! Not because I was going home early (that was a bonus) but the fact that I was right and my dad should have believed me! Greg is always right!

About an hour later, my dad came to collect me. This time he'd managed to get to school in his car, and we headed straight to Gran Hopper's house... just as I'd predicted a few days prior.

Mama Rosa

As I was growing up, my mother and father owned a gorgeous Italian restaurant in our home town of Bishop Auckland. It was slap bang in the market place only a few steps from Auckland Castle. I always thought I was a real-life princess living so close to the castle. It was such a busy restaurant, always full of hustle and bustle especially on Thursdays, Fridays and Saturday nights. I was lucky because I lived half of the week above the restaurant whilst my parents worked downstairs, and the other half either with my grandparents or in our little cottage that was just a few miles away from Mama Rosa.

I loved being at the restaurant. I fondly remember the checked green and white table cloths, the old chianti wine bottles with red melted candles stuck in the top, the smell of garlic bread wafting through the place, the dusty fake grapes draped along the bar, the turning dessert canopy displaying my mother's famous Crème de Menthe gateaux, and, of course, the sound of the lambada song blasting from the stereo system.

Saturdays were my favourite. They would often start with a visit to the local cash and carry with my father, to stock up on the

booze for the bar in the restaurant. We'd
also buy big jars of olives and massive tins
of tomatoes. We'd get back to the
restaurant and food prep time would start.
I remember having a stool right next to the
prep bench! I'd watch my mother chop
mushrooms, peppers, ham - all of the faffy
stuff - so it was all ready for when Mr B
entered the building.

Mr B was a funny character, he was very,
very Italian. "Ciao Bella" he would shout at
the top of his voice whenever he saw me.
He was small in height with a massive
belly, and he always wore a white chef's hat
and matching white apron with 'Mr B'
embroidered at the top left-hand corner. He
had a booming voice and was so bossy with
the girls – our waitresses, who became
more like my parents' adopted children.
They'd all stroll in at about five o'clock to
help get the tables set up for the evening. I
fondly remember my dad giving them a pep
talk just before the doors opened for
another busy night.

Because the days and nights were long and
busy my dad always had a radiator nap
before service began. Underneath the long

narrow restaurant window there was a huge radiator, and each day my dad moved the tables surrounding it and he'd have a half an hour nap on the radiator. No pillow or blanket or anything like that. He'd just close his eyes and drift off. I remember joining him on many occasions and even now to this day nothing beats a radiator power nap!

The Colourful Mama Rosa Customers

We had a lot of regular customers in the restaurant, who would come in at the same time every week and order the same food, and they were all lovely. Two customers in particular were my favourite. Graham and Liliana were hippies who spent some of their time in the UK and the rest in Goa. Liliana was Indian, with gorgeous long dark wavy hair right down to her knees, and the darkest of eyes. She always wore brightly coloured outfits, and was dripping in beautiful jewellery and crystals. Graham looked like Jesus with his wavy shoulder length hair and long beard. He wore big, baggy yoga pants, flip flops (Jesus sandals) and crisp white grandad shirts which complimented his tanned skin perfectly.

He wore an amethyst crystal around his neck on a leather strap, and wacky friendship bracelets. I was besotted with them both.

One night they walked through the restaurant doors (late as usual) and ordered their half carafe of red wine and vegetarian pizza to share. Because it was quiet in the restaurant, I was allowed downstairs. I remember the music was loud and one of the girls lifted me up to sit on the bar. In the heat of the moment, I decided to jump, thinking Jana was going to catch me. Big mistake. I fell and bashed my head on the floor tiles. Oh, my goodness did I scream!

Graham and Liliana jumped out of their seats, and ran over. Graham put a hand on my forehead and Liliana put her hand on the huge lump that was sticking out the back of my head. My tears stopped immediately. I began to see all kinds of purples, violets, and indigo colours – the psychedelic kind – swirling in front of my face.

Then Graham looked at me, looked at my dad and said, "She's an indigo child, Anthony."

"What the hell are you talking about, man?" said my dad.

"She's an indigo child. She can see things other people can't." He took the amethyst necklace off and said to me, "If you're ever in pain, or feel lonely, just hold this." And still to this day I do.

Chapter 2 ~ The Adventures of the Babysitters

"I'm not weird! I'm limited edition."

My parents used to work so hard in the restaurant – they were there morning, noon and night – and a lot of the time, I would just go to bed and watch TV or read, so they didn't really need anyone to babysit me. Instead, Dad and me used our walkie talkies to keep in touch and obviously someone would keep popping upstairs to check I was ok. I have great memories of sitting in bed and listening to the music, laughter and hustle and bustle from the restaurant downstairs.

There was one occasion where, unfortunately, I was left unattended and my mam got concerned after she could hear the loo flushing constantly over a period of half an hour or so. She shouted up the stairs to ask if I was ok, and then when I didn't answer, I heard her sprint up the stairs.

"Oh, my god, what the hell have you done, Keely? Go downstairs right now and show your dad what you've done."

I walked downstairs, with a fistful of hair and sheepishly looked at my dad.

"What the hell have you done?" he said.

"I've cut my hair."

"Why?"

"Because Greg said."

"Oh my God, I am sick of hearing about Greg. This has got to stop."

Funnily enough, I wasn't allowed to stay on my own upstairs after that, and so that's when my parents started getting a babysitter for me. The girls who used to work for my parents in Mama Rosa were always around, and because they were treated like part of the family, they would often babysit me.

Now you'd think finding a babysitter would be easy, what with all these young girls eager to earn some extra cash. But things in my life aren't always as straightforward as you might think. And I managed to work my way through quite a few babysitters.

Babysitter 1 - Linzi

It was a dark, cold winter night when Linzi came over to babysit. She was a gorgeous, lovely girl with big, bright red lips. She was training to be an air hostess, so you can imagine how glamorous she was. Well, when it came to my bedtime, she tried her best to get me to bed. But I wanted to sit up and talk to this lovely girl. Being the gobshite I am, I kicked up a bit of a fuss as I stomped my way up the stairs.

She started following me.

"You can't go up there. Greg's there," I said.

"What do you mean?" she replied, looking puzzled.

"He's told me he doesn't like you," I replied.

"Well, where is he?" She began to look scared.

"He's under my bed, take a look."

"No, I can't."

"Oh, hang on he's outside looking at you through the window."

"That's it, I'm going to have to ring your mam and dad. You're really scaring me, Keely."

True to her word, she rang the restaurant and they had to come home. She explained how I'd told her about Greg following her around, and that she was scared and just wanted to go home.

Poor Linzi. I don't think she ever got over that night. She never looked after me again, despite my parents asking her many times.

Funnily enough, my parents bumped into her recently, and Greg's name came up straightaway (even 25 years on). I clearly had freaked her out!

Babysitter 2 – Vicky

The next-door neighbour, an old lady in her early 70s with senile dementia, was babysitter number 2. Why my parents even considered her I do not know. She was a bit of a hypochondriac and would always say, "I've got diverticulitis."

Greg said, "Give her some smarties and tell her they're tablets that will fix her diverticulitis."

So I did. She asked me to get her some tonic water, which I did, and I watched her swallow about 5 smarties in one go. She went for a nap and then later in the day, she popped into our house and started dancing round the room saying,

"Keely and Greg have cured my diverticulitis! I'm cured!"

She may have been slightly batty, but she wasn't easily fazed. I would often tell her that Greg was sitting next to her, but her reply was always unexpected.

"Hi Greg."

And Greg would look at me and roll his eyes, and say, "cuckoo".

But I was desperate for Mam and Dad to come home so I could escape from her. I remember telling her that my parents were going to be in a car accident, so she had to ring them and ask them to come home. Of course, this wasn't true.

It was past closing time and my parents still hadn't come home and she couldn't get hold of them. So she rang the hospitals and the police... all because 'Greg said' there was going to be an accident. When they eventually came home, I was laughing, Vicky was crying because she thought they were going to die in a car accident and she blurted the whole story out.

"I thought you were lying in a ditch somewhere."

That night I got into big trouble. My dad tucked me into bed and said,

"Keely, you have got to stop doing this. It's getting out of hand."

One time, when we lived at Etherley Grange, we went to her house and I remember it smelled foisty. She had photographs all over her walls (she was a well-travelled woman) and when she caught me looking at one of her pictures, she said,

"That's my late husband, Keely."

"He didn't love you. He had another girlfriend," I replied.

Her face dropped. "How do you know that then?"

"Greg said."

Obviously, I got another telling off but years later, my mam did confirm to me that her husband had left her for another woman and that could have been the cause of her mental health problems later in life.

Babysitter 3 – Catherine

Catherine was another of the Mama Rosa waitresses. She became one of the closest to my family. I was her bridesmaid when she eventually got married, and she became my sister's nanny. I've always got on well with Catherine because we're on the same spiritual wavelength, and she's always been psychic herself. Plus, she just gets me.

Catherine was one of my favourite babysitters because she would come upstairs to look after me and we could talk about anything and everything spiritual. Although she never saw Greg, she used to pick up on the spirits who also resided in Mama Rosa.

One of the strangest things to happen to Catherine and me was when we dreamt about exactly the same thing on exactly the same night. When she came into work the next day she mentioned to my dad that she'd dreamt about a secret room upstairs inside the attic.

"This is what Keely's been saying to me this morning. I have no idea what you're talking about, but I know for a fact there are no other rooms. I've got the deeds to the building and I know there's only one attic room," my dad said.

But we weren't as easily convinced. Because we'd had the same dream about this secret room, on exactly the same night, we asked my dad if we could go upstairs before service started that night. Thankfully, he agreed.

We got our torches and went on an adventure up the stairs. We got up to the attic and Greg said, "It's in there," and pointed to a wall.

"It's in there, Dad," I repeated.

"Bloody can't be in there, man, that's a stone wall." And as he tapped on it his face dropped. The wall was paper thin. So he ran downstairs, grabbed a hammer and started knocking down the wall. Behind that wall, there was, just as we'd predicted another staircase leading to the secret room. It was only the size of a cubby hole, but it was still a room. Once again, I'd manage to freak my dad out, this time with Catherine's help too.

When the babysitters dried up, or when my parents were having a rare night out away from the restaurant, I would go to Gran Hopper's house. Gran Hopper, like my dad, wasn't a big believer in the unconventional. Although, looking back, I know she always had a sixth sense, but I don't think she would necessarily believe in ghosts or spirit, or anything she couldn't physically see or touch.

I have many memories from Gran Hopper's house. Once I can remember standing at the top of the stairs and trying to switch off the light, but I couldn't reach it. Then this angel, what I can only describe as a beam of light, floated over to me from nowhere, picked me up and carried me down the stairs. This was the first time of many that this would happen, but it still puzzles me to this day how I got from top to bottom.

I used to love dancing and putting on shows for anyone who would watch, and I enjoyed many years at dancing school as a child. Grandad Hopper always used to encourage me to dance and he'd always put *Boney M* on his record player for me.

"Who are you dancing for, Keely?" he would ask.

"All the old people sat on the empty chairs."

I should explain here that my Gran and Grandad had 10 children, and so there were always spare chairs hanging around for impromptu family gatherings. What they didn't know was that whenever I was there, I could see old people sitting on the chairs – they were all see-through, just like Greg. They would clap for me when I finished my dancing shows. One really old, eccentric man, wore a tall black hat and held a walking cane. He looked like an undertaker. Every time I finished dancing, he would tap his cane on the floor and say,

"Bravo, Keely, bravo." I thought I was the best dancer in the world.

Gran Hopper was always trying to get me to go outside and play with the other kids in the street, and could never understand how I could be happy alone and indoors. But I had my see-through people, didn't I? I didn't need anyone else to play with.

She wasn't too happy with me being under her feet all the time, though, particularly when I was being kind to the see-through people. I would get the Mellow Birds out of the cupboard, and the whisk, and the milk, and mix it all up in a big bowl. Then I'd get the ladle and pour the frothy coffee out for all the see-through people, leaving all the slops on the benches, no milk, and an empty coffee jar.

Grandad Hopper was a lovely man, he had allotments and was a big gardener. On a Sunday night, he would make a big salad, with scally onions, apples, carrot, tomatoes, cucumber and cold potatoes left over from lunch. I would sit under the table while he ate his Sunday evening salad and pinch lettuce from his plate, to feed to the see-through children I was sitting with under the table. Luckily, they were lovely people and must have had the patience of saints. Grandad Hopper would just laugh at my antics, and roll his eyes occasionally. I knew I was always his blue-eyed girl and I loved him to bits – still do.

As a young girl, I didn't realise Grandad Hopper was really quite spooky himself. He was very good at pregnancy predictions, and the gender of a baby – and never got it wrong. Apparently, when my mam and Aunty Alison were pregnant together (they both had babies within two weeks of each other) my grandad had told them one was having a girl and the other a boy. But he wished it was the other way around. Nobody understood what he meant at first but then it clicked. My grandparents had ten children, but the Hopper name was never carried on because my dad and his brother all had daughters.

Babysitter 4 – Aunty Jilly

A few doors up from our lovely little cottage in Etherley lived a wonderful lady whom I called Aunty Jilly. She was in her sixties but didn't look a day over forty. She was such a very glamorous woman with her striking bottle-blonde hair and trademark bright red Chanel lipstick.

Aunty Jilly had a very privileged upbringing and I adored hearing stories about her wealthy childhood, travelling the world and going to finishing school in Switzerland. I would listen to her for hours. She had certainly been a wild one in her day.

What I remember most about Aunty Jilly was her love of parties. I fondly remember her drinks cabinet in the corner of her living room, too. It was filled to the rafters with pretty wine and whisky bottles and I can still hear the 'ching ching' of her expensive crystal glasses and tumblers. She would let me sip some of her Indian tonic water from a thickly cut whisky glass with pretty diamond patterns on it, whilst she lit up a menthol cigarette and smoked it from a long black cigarette holder like Cruella de Vil.

She had numerous lighters and I used to watch her flick them into life with her long, red polished nails. The other thing I always remember about Aunty Jilly was that she loved cats. She had three black and white ones and whenever you went into her house, they'd always be sat close to her. Each Christmas and New Year our family would be invited over for a party. Obviously, because I was still young I'd only be allowed to stay for a little while but I remember sitting in her window seat amongst the posh royal blue velvet cushions and admiring the buffet.

"Why does she always have midget food, Mam?" I must have asked that questions hundreds of times over the years.

"Because it's posh," said my mam, every time. Even to this day I still believe that the smaller the food the posher it must be! She would have trays of baby eggs with frog spawn all over them, I later found out that this was quails egg and caviar!

"Don't spit it into a napkin Keely, they are delightful," she would say as I was just about to hurl my guts up into a thick, festive, freshly pressed napkin.

If my mam was ever busy doing the washing or cleaning the house, I'd often pop down to Aunty Jilly's for a change of scenery. A quick little visit just to see if she was ok, and maybe listen to one of her magical stories about some posh party she'd been to or some wonderful country she'd visited.

One day I popped down to her house, knocked on the door twice and let myself in because she'd always told me I could do that if the gate was open.

"Hello, Keely," she said in her lovely voice. "I was hoping you'd pop by today, I want to show you something." In that moment she bent down by the side of her armchair and produced this gorgeous black jewellery box. It was fairly big in size and had beautiful, red oriental flowers on it.

"I bought this in China, Keely. Open it up and take a look." And I did just that. Wow. There were heaps of beautiful necklaces, rings and brooches. I'd like you to have these, Keely. You can wear them when you are a big girl."

Oh, my goodness, I thought. I remember filling up with tears and I even had a shivery lip as if I was going to burst out crying because I was so overwhelmed by her kind gesture. Just then, one of our other neighbours walked in and I managed to pull myself together. Now, I don't want to name this person or go into any detail about her but put it this way I had never ever liked her. Every time I saw her I felt uneasy. She had a look.

My parents would say, "Keely why don't you like her?" or "Keely, be polite and say hello" when we saw her. But there was always something niggling away at me whenever she came near.

When I was in my yard one day playing in my Wendy house with Greg, he told me that she was an evil woman who had been to prison in her last life. He also told me that she was trying to poison her family. I didn't know whether she was a real-life witch, but one thing is for certain, I wasn't going to give her the time of day, whether I was five years old or fifty-five!

Anyway, back to Aunty Jilly's jewellery box. After spending quite a while looking at all the beautiful jewels, I decided to take a necklace with a pearl on it, a ring with a

ruby red stone because I had earrings to
match it, and a beautiful gold brooch in the
shape of a cat with teeny tiny diamond
studs around its collar... I loved it! She also
gave me a little make-up bag full of hair
clips and velvet scrunchy bobbles that
would look lovely with my dancing
costumes. I was over the moon. I couldn't
believe she had given me these special
treasures. In that moment I'd already
decided I would make her a thank you card
with my new Crayola scented pens!

"Thank you so much," I said and jumped
up to give her a cuddle.

"Off you go then, dear," she said in her
calming voice.

And off I went skipping back up the lane to
tell my mam all about it. But something
didn't feel right again. I was going 'funny'.
My tummy was all swirly and I felt like my
heart was going to escape out of my chest.
Greg popped up.

"Run faster, Keely,'" he said. I tried to
speed up but somehow tripped over my
little feet. Stood behind me was the 'other'
neighbour, the nasty one!

"I'll take those," she said and snatched the bag of hair bobbles. "They won't look very nice on you. They will suit my granddaughter far better. And I'll have those as well," she said and grabbed the necklace and ring from my tiny hand.

"You are nasty!" I said to her. "Greg doesn't like you. You are a witch!"' I remember trembling and the fact that a bit of blood was trickling down my leg made me feel worse. I scrambled up from the floor and ran the few paces to my front door.

"Have you been falling over again, Keely?" asked my mam.

"That nasty neighbour took my stuff from me. Greg said she was a witch," I replied between the tears.

It's not that my mam didn't believe me but I don't think she actually realised how much Aunty Jilly had given me that day or how nasty our other neighbour was. As the years went by at Etherley Grange, all the grown-ups eventually began to realise what a nasty piece of work our evil neighbour was. It turns out that on Aunty Jilly's death bed she was actually stealing money from her purse, and taking her belongings to sell.

One thing that day taught me is that whenever I get the 'swirly washing machine tummy' then I instantly know that someone has a very nasty streak, and to this day I always listen to it. It never ever fails me.

Chapter 3 ~ School Days - The Convent

"I am the resurrection and the life. Anyone who believes in me will live, even after dying. Everyone who lives in me and believes in me will never ever die."

~ Bible

Throughout my years at primary school, I excelled in all subjects, and I loved every minute of being at Escomb Primary. It was a gorgeous, quaint school with lots of kind and warm teachers – all of whom I loved. To this day I'm still in touch with a lot of my Escomb schoolfriends and I have happy memories of being there.

The only fault my teachers could find with me, apparently, was that I struggled to concentrate. I was a daydreamer – who would think that?! Obviously, this is because of Greg, and the see-through people, but I couldn't explain that to my teachers, really, could I?

Because of this lack of concentration, the fact that I was doing really well at school and my parents wanting to encourage this, they sent me to a convent in a nearby village called Wolsingham. St Anne's was an independent, private, all-girls school, run and taught by nuns (the Sisters of Mercy). There were some mainstream teachers, too, but generally, most of our lessons were taught by nuns.

It was 1996 when I started secondary school, and what a shock it was. To go from my happy school with smiley, friendly teachers and lots of friends, to the complete opposite, was pretty scary, I can tell you.

Crucifixes, statues and paintings of Jesus, Mary and the saints filled every wall and corridor of the school. In the hall was a huge wooden cross (about six feet high) with Jesus nailed to it, wearing his crown of thorns and blood dripping down his face. For any little girl or boy who was new to this religious institution - with its strict rules, incense, mass, sacraments, rosary beads and Hail Marys – it meant a completely different way of schooling to what they'd previously known.

For five years of my life I had to wear this awful brown and yellow uniform – brown tights and knickers, a yellow shirt and a brown jumper with yellow embroidery around the v-neck. We had indoor and outdoor shoes, which had to be brown (obviously), and in summer the uniform changed to a yellow petticoat and a straw hat. We had brown satchels and wicker cookery baskets, and for PE we had to wear yellow t-shirts and yellow gym knickers, with a tennis skirt. It didn't just look horrendous, it also felt scratchy on your skin, too.

Even during the first week I knew I was going to hate the convent. I know every school needs rules and children need discipline but to me, this place had an awful feel about it. We had to go into mass each morning (with our indoor shoes on), repeat our Hail Marys and sit through awful assemblies.

The school was always cold – you could literally see your breath in the winter – and I always wondered why, if my parents were paying thousands of pounds a year to provide me with a good education, couldn't they put the heating on in this hell hole?

After assembly we would all head off to our classroom, and line up outside the door and wait for the teacher to arrive. The nun (or teacher) would arrive and tell us to enter the classroom, but we couldn't sit down until we'd said 'good morning' and were instructed to do so. During the lesson if any adult entered the classroom, we all had to stand up and say, 'good morning' or 'good afternoon' in our best sing-song voices. But when we stood up we had to be silent, or make as little noise as possible.

One of the nuns, Sister Anthony, used to regularly tell me off for making a scraping noise with my chair when I stood up. "Empty vessels make the most noise," she would say every time. Empty vessel indeed!

I hated most of my lessons – except cookery, art, and geography – I don't know if the teachers of these subjects were the nicest ones, and more empathic towards me, or whether I was just generally interested in these subjects. Anyhow, these were the only lessons I felt comfortable in each week.

The art room was right at the top of the building, and I always felt safe there. This was probably because there were so many see-through people lurking around. Some of my friends used to be scared of going up to the art room, but to me it was like coming home.

The building was very old – it was established in 1892 – so you can imagine how much spirit activity there was. The old spirit nuns used to wander around the building, and walk the corridors of the convent. They always looked sad for some reason, as though they were stuck between worlds – or heaven and hell. One used to drag a cross along the floor, and although I wasn't particularly frightened by this sight, despite it looking like the beginning of a horror movie, I would just feel incredibly sorry for her.

There was also a little girl called Mary. She had long, dark hair with a centre parting and was wearing a nightdress, and she became good pals with Greg. She told him that she had been there forever. I can also remember another nun who used to pace backwards and forwards across the stage –

and this was rumoured amongst the children who were boarders there before my time (from 1985 St Anne's was just a day school but prior to that it had been a boarding school as well).

Many different ghost stories had emerged over the years, and I always used to laugh to myself when I saw the scared faces listening to the storytellers. It wasn't the stories they needed to worry about. The children should have been more concerned with the ghosts and spirits living in the art room! But of course, I didn't tell anyone.

I remember when some girls did a Ouija board in the library. How they managed to get away with it, I don't know. They made their own makeshift Ouija board using pieces of paper with numbers on to represent the alphabet, and placed a glass in the middle. The tables in the library were huge, they were the old textile tables, and you could easily sit ten girls around them.

So they started with the Ouija board – I wasn't there but I heard the story later – and apparently the glass had been flung off the table and smashed to pieces on the floor, and a girl was thrown from one side of the table to the other.

If only they had known what they were dealing with, they would never have diced with something so dangerous. The energy that was hidden in the walls, to me, seemed very dark. Greg would tell me to keep away from it all, and I did, but I always had this gut feeling that people had been tortured in the library – which used to be the boarders' bedrooms. My skin would literally crawl every time I walked into the library, and I could never get out quick enough.

One subject I completely despised was maths. Mrs Hartley was my maths teacher, and looked like an Abba throwback with her blonde flicked-out hair and huge Deidre Barlow specs. She had no patience with me. In fact, Greg told me that from the very first time I met her I would never get on with her and I would never like her. I remember my mam coming back from a parents' evening once in floods of tears. Mrs Hartley had told her that I would never amount to anything.

I've learned two valuable lessons about maths and numbers - one from my dad who told me to put a pound sign at the front of any number for it to make sense, and the other lesson is to ask Google. We can find out anything we want these days, can't we?

All joking aside, however, I would advise anyone who does struggle with maths, not to worry about it. Just take your time, find someone who can teach you patiently about the things you're stuck with, and you'll find your way. Maths isn't the be all and end all. I still haven't used algebra or a scientific calculator since my school days.

As you can imagine, I used to dread going into maths, and whenever we stood outside the classroom I would feel sick with dread. One of Mrs Hartley's favourite catchphrases was, "You can't carry a calculator wherever you go!" Ha, well, I've got news for you, Mrs Hartley, welcome to the age of technology and phone calculators!

Chapter 4 ~ Matthew and The Curse of The Curly Wurly

"I do all of my own stunts."

I first met Matthew in the summer of 1996 when I was just 12 years old. I had moved to a new house in Bishop Auckland and when we arrived in the removal van, Matthew and his friends were in the neighbour's garden playing football.

When we pulled up on the drive, I said to my mam, "I'm going to marry him."

"Keely, who are you talking about? Who are you going to marry?"

"Him there, the tall one."

"Keely, you're 12 years old, how the heck do you know you're going to marry him? You don't even know his name."

At this time, Matthew was 12 and already about 6 foot tall. He was just gorgeous. He reminded me of John Travolta and my favourite film, was, yes you've guessed it,

Grease! I jumped out of the removal van and decided to introduce myself. I can't remember what I said but I can definitely remember going into the garden and talking to them. They must have thought I was absolutely crackers. Funny enough, the boys he was playing with are still Matthew's best friends to this day and we still spend a lot of time with them.

I remember my dad unloading the removal van and saying to us, "Don't get too comfy, girls. I'm not having you two living next door to lots of boys." And true to his word, 18 months later, we left that lovely house and moved to a remote farm in the middle of nowhere. Dads, eh?!

Me and the boys next door spent the whole of that summer together. We played football, and rounders, we had water fights, and generally just hung around getting to know each other. Every time I saw Matthew I fell a little bit more in love with him.

He has since told me that he felt the same. Obviously, he wasn't telling everyone that he was going to marry me (he wasn't as full on as me, ha!) and he always kept his cards close to his chest, but he knew deep down that there was a strong (and pretty strange) connection between us. I say 'strange' because from the first moment I clapped eyes on Matthew, I felt like I'd known him all my life.

And Greg has said the same. He's told me on more than one occasion that Matthew and me had been married in a previous life, and that he had been our son. Obviously, I didn't let on to Matthew at this stage.

About a year after first meeting Matthew, he, sadly, went through some painful times. He lost his father and, understandably, really struggled with this. When you're young and going through trauma, it is a natural reaction to try and find yourself. His childhood took on a whole different direction, and we lost contact. But I still thought about him every day. And, of course I had Greg in my ear telling me that our paths would most definitely cross again.

Something I should point out here, is that I never met Matthew's dad. He lived about 20 miles away and rarely came to Bishop

Auckland. I didn't even see a photograph of
him until much later into our relationship.
But when we were about 17, I described
Matthew's dad to an absolute tee. I told
Matthew about his stonewashed blue jeans,
the way he wore his hair, and I even
described the kind of bomber jacket he had
worn before his passing. I'd described the
way his house was decorated and the type
of plates they used to eat from. Matthew
knew there was no way I could have known
any of this. He told me later that my
accuracy had really blown him away.

Anyway, fast forward three or four years
and I'd started an apprenticeship with a
local travel agent in Bishop Auckland.
During my lunchbreak one day, I bumped
into James, who was Matthew's best friend,
and the boy I'd briefly lived next door to. He
told me Matthew had joined the army. My
heart sank.

"Tell him I'm asking after him, would you?"
I said, and for some reason I assumed
Matthew must have had a girlfriend at this
point.

"Yea, course I will," James replied. And that was that.

Greg told me to play it cool and although inside I was desperate to find out all the juicy details about Matthew's life, I did what Greg said. Two weeks later, and totally out of the blue, I received a text from Matthew. I was smiling from ear to ear.

Hi, it's Nixon. James said you were asking after me, and I thought I'd say hi. Hope you don't mind him passing on your number.

Mind? Mind? No way did I mind! I was ecstatic to hear from him again after all this time.

Another two weeks passed and we'd been texting non-stop. It was my 16th birthday and we had a big party planned at the farm. The DJ was booked, the invites were sent, and Matthew was home, so he came to the party with some of our friends. From that point, we were inseparable.

But army life got in the way. He was based down in Chatham in Kent in those days, and we never saw each other for 6 weeks at a time. As you can imagine, the phone bills were huge. My whole £60 weekly wage contributed to my phone bill and Dad picked up the rest – he wasn't very happy!

Looking back, although our 6-week separations seemed too hard to cope with, it was only the tip of the iceberg. Matthew ended up being sent all over the world with the army – Iraq, Jordan, Afghanistan, Germany, Canada and most of the UK – which meant we sometimes had to spend months and months apart.

In 2003, when I was 18, Matthew and me got engaged. It wasn't a traditional proposal, and obviously you can't propose to a psychic because they already know what's going to happen! But this one day, I knew Matthew had something in his pocket and I was hell bent on finding out what it was.

"What's in your pocket? I know you've got something in there, Matthew."

"Nothing. What are you talking about?"

"Tell me what's in your pocket."

"Oh, God, Keely. It's a ring, all right? I was going to ask you to marry me tonight.

There's never any surprises with you around, is there?"

"Oh, were you?" I said, trying to be all coy, despite scuppering his plans.

"Yes, I was."

"Well, the answer's yes. I'd love to marry you!"

Four years later, on the 15th February, 2008, we eloped to Gretna Green, just the two of us. I put on my wedding dress in the toilets in the services. My dress didn't fit properly so I stuffed some loo roll down my bra, put on a bit of lippy, and we had a cup of tea together before the marriage ceremony began. Although it was perfect, it wasn't quite like the fairy-tale wedding I'd imagined as a child, when I lived in Mama Rosa and thought I was a princess.

Matthew was still in the army at this point, but I didn't really want to be an army wife. I wanted to stay close to my family. It wouldn't have made sense for me to move miles away with Matthew because I would have been left all alone when he went on tour anyway. Having my family close to me was very important too.

We've been so lucky in that Matthew and me are soulmates, because it means that despite being thousands of miles away, on and off for the first five years of our marriage, we got through it. We've had some scary adventures along the way, though.

The Curse of the Curly Wurly

Now this might sound like I've lost my marbles here but bear with me. Matthew has had quite a few accidents over the years and they all begin when he eats a certain kind of chocolate bar.

Yes, the good old Curly Wurly. It may seem harmless enough but believe me, I have banned Matthew from eating them. Let me explain.

Curly Wurly Incident #1

It was a red hot Sunday. Me and Matthew were about 17 years old, and I'd just passed my driving test so I was totally loving life and my newfound independence. My dad asked if we would nip to the local garage to get some milk and a newspaper for him while he painted the wooden garage door.

We jumped in the car, and I got a funny feeling. I can only describe it as a tickle in my gut. You'll know by now that means something bad was about to happen.

"I think we're going to have an accident, Matthew."

"Stop talking nonsense, Keely."

"No, I've just got this feeling. I think we're going to crash the car."

"You're crackers, you. We'll see," he replied and rolled his eyes. We popped into the garage, bought my dad's milk and paper, I grabbed a Kinder Bueno and Matthew grabbed a Curly Wurly. I set off to drive the short journey home, with Darius belting out *Colour Blind*. I loved that song! For anyone who isn't old enough to know who Darius is, he was on a programme called *Pop Idol* which preceded *X-Factor*.

So far so good. There wasn't much traffic on the road, so I was starting to doubt my gut feeling. Maybe I'd been wrong and my swirly tummy meant something else was going to happen instead.

We pulled round the corner to the lane. Yipee, we'd made it back home! I drove slowly towards the sloping drive, and spotted my dad who was just finishing off painting the last section of the garage door. He looked well pleased with himself. Then just as I thought we were out of the woods, I pressed the brakes to slow down and nothing. I tried again. I tried pumping the brakes. Nothing happened.

The car rolled straight towards the freshly painted gates next to the garage door, and we got came crashing to a stop. My little Ford Ka took the gates off their hinges, smoke started billowing out of the bonnet, and I didn't know whether to laugh or cry.

"What have you done to my gates?" my dad shouted.

Now 15 years on, I am allowed to laugh at this story and it's one my dad often repeats to anyone who'll listen.

Curly Wurly Incident #2

At this point we hadn't made the Curly Wurly connection but when Matthew had another accident a couple of months later, just after he'd ate a Curly Wurly, I put two and two together. Matthew had been on exercise, when he'd slipped into a ditch and broken his ankle. He was on crutches for weeks but the upside was that at least he got to come home for a while.

I said to Matthew while we were watching TV one night, "Have you ever noticed that every time you have a Curly Wurly, you have an accident?"

"No, funny enough I hadn't noticed that. You are completely crackers for even thinking that."

Curly Wurly Incident #3

Now that I'd planted the Curly Wurly seed in Matthew's head, he wanted to push the boundaries. He rang me up from work one day for our usual lunchtime chit-chat.

"I've had a chicken burger for lunch today and guess what I had for afters."

"No idea... what?"

"Two Curly Wurlys."

"Oh, Matthew what have I told you about eating Curly Wurlys?"

Later that day, just after I'd returned home from work, I checked my phone. Four missed calls from Matthew's mam. The panic set in. Matthew had been rushed into hospital from the back of an army truck. He was in the operating theatre having pins put into his leg, from his ankle to his knee and then from his knee to his hip. Yes, he had managed to break his leg in three different places.

After his surgery, me and Matthew's mam drove to Harrogate hospital to see him. All I can remember is shouting at him about eating Curly Wurlys. He told me I was a witch and that I'd cursed him. It was, naturally, all my fault.

Curly Wurly Incident #4 and the Return of the Angels

Matthew had been posted to Afghanistan and was there for about three months when I started to get my funny feeling.

Prior to this I'd felt fine and Greg would always tell me that Matthew was fine and would return home safely. But on this particular day I couldn't shake off this awful feeling. I couldn't get comfortable. I kept being sick. I was sweating. I couldn't sit down or stand up. In fact, I didn't really know what to do with myself.

I rang my mam and she thought I might be coming down with 'flu. So, thinking that this was probably the reason why I felt so out of sorts, I took myself off to bed. I laid there, drifting in and out of sleep. I heard footsteps coming up the stairs – they sounded like Matthew's but he was thousands of miles away. The bedroom door opened and a pure white energy floated around the bed, kissed me on the cheek, and said,

"He'll be ok, you know. Don't worry."

I remember trying to open my eyes but they felt too heavy.

"You can't open your eyes," the voice said, "because you're not supposed to see this." I tried and tried to prise my eyes open, but they felt like lead. I was desperate to see what they were talking about. In my mind's eye I could see all this white energy in the shape of a twister or tornado moving around the room. I could hear beautiful chanting telling me "He's ok, he's ok, he's ok," and then the white energy vanished.

I went into a really deep sleep then, and the next morning I woke up and, strangely, felt fine. I checked my phone and there had been a few missed calls and a voice message from Matthew. He wanted me to know that there had been a massive explosion and one of his friends had died. He was getting some shrapnel removed from his leg but he was ok, apart from being heartbroken about his friend.

Later, I discovered that his mam had sent him a care package (food parcel to you and me) and guess what was in it? Yep, a Curly Wurly.

Can you understand why Curly Wurly is actually a swear word in our house?

Chapter 5 ~ My Babies

"An angel in the book of life, wrote down my baby's birth then whispered as she closed the book, 'Too beautiful for earth." ♡

I'll be honest, this isn't going to be easy for me to write as even now, to this day, my eyes fill up with tears and my heart aches that little bit more, but I'll give it a go.

Back in early April 2011, whilst on a mini-break at the seaside, I felt funny. I'd not felt right for weeks, it was a mixture of my swirly stomach feeling (where something wasn't right with the world) and sickness... lots of sickness! I felt utterly exhausted and remember lying in bed with no energy whatsoever. For days I'd put it down to eating something dodgy or a tummy bug or the onset of 'flu.

Pull yourself together, Keely, and have some fun, I kept telling myself. And I did just that. Even though I felt rough I forced myself on the rides at Flamingo Land. We went to the water park and I danced with my little cousin at the clubhouse disco because I didn't want to let her down! I just got on with it.

The following day we were due to go home anyway and I'd been thinking about booking a doctor's appointment. I was sure I had some sort of kidney or bladder infection brewing - I couldn't stop peeing. All the signs of pregnancy were there but at the time I just didn't put two and two together. I kept thinking my period was coming as each time I'd gone to the toilet I was wiping blood.

As we drove back from the Yorkshire Moors, I felt ill. We had to stop a few times, for me to go to the loo, and get another bag of ready salted crisps (something I'd been fancying regularly for weeks). As I got back in the car, Matthew was sat looking like a Cheshire Cat with a big greasy-spoon cheese burger and onions dripping down the sides of the bread.

"Oh my God, Matthew, that's disgusting," I said.

"No it's not, it's gorgeous, do you want a bite?" he asked.

"I'll pass, thanks," I replied as I could feel my mouth watering up with vomit! "I'm going to throw up," I said, as I opened the car door and emptied my insides out on to the pavement. After pulling myself together we set off for home again, and I jumped in the back seat to try and sleep off my nausea.

As I drifted off, Greg appeared out of the blue. "You need a wee stick," he smiled and within a flash he was gone again. A wee stick? What did he mean? My mind ticked over for a couple of seconds. Ah a pregnancy test!

"Matthew, Greg says I need a wee stick, I think he means a pregnancy test!"

"That would explain a lot," he said calmly. "We'll go and get one now."

As soon as I got home I did the test. And it was positive. I was pregnant. I was excited and nervous at the same time with a streak of relief that I hadn't been feeling like shit for no reason at all.

Now the strangest thing was I didn't see Greg for the next couple of months... it was like he was hiding away and I didn't know why.

Our family and friends were over the moon that we were expecting and within the space of a few days our news started to spread. I went to see my GP who told me I'd need a check-up and a scan in a few weeks. I couldn't wait.

After weeks and weeks of feeling ill I started to feel a little better, I was eleven weeks pregnant and my sickness was starting to subside a bit. I was so pleased to be able to eat something without wanting to throw it all back up!

Throughout my pregnancy I'd had spots of blood but I'd heard this could be totally normal so I didn't worry too much. I'd gone to my first midwife appointment on my own, as Matthew was over in Germany with work at the time. She took my bloods and arranged for a scan for the following day because of the bleeding. I was so excited yet so nervous. I wanted to be happy, but my tummy was doing the washing machine thing that it always does when something isn't right.

Because Matthew was away, I asked my sister, Emily, to pop along to the scan with me. Whilst I was in the waiting area I felt awful, my heart was racing and I couldn't settle. A few couples had come out of the sonography room looking so happy. They couldn't take their eyes off their scan pictures.

"Keely Potts," shouted the sonographer, "would you like to come through?" We went in and I explained about the blood.

"Try not to worry, a lot of people have spotting in early pregnancy," she replied, as she put the freezing cold jelly on my tummy. She probed the scanning stick over my tiny bump and I saw her face drop. My heart sank. I knew something wasn't right. Tears pricked my eyes.

"I'm sorry," she said, and she moved the monitor further round so I could see it. "Here's your baby." She pointed out everything on the screen. "But look at the heartbeat, it's a tiny flicker of a beat." Those were her exact words. My baby was slowly dying inside of me and there was nothing they could do. Go home and rest

was the advice she gave me, come back and
see me next week and we will see if there's
any change. I sobbed and sobbed. What did
I do to deserve this? I was exactly twelve
weeks pregnant that day. We drove back
home. All I wanted to do was climb into bed
and cry. I wanted my husband home too
but unfortunately the army wouldn't send
him back, so I crawled into bed and got as
much rest as I could.

A few days passed and there was no change
in me, everything just felt the same. I kept
going over everything in my mind. Maybe
the sonographer had got something wrong,
maybe I'd go back in a few more days and
my baby's heartbeat would be going at the
speed it should be, I'd Googled and read up
on miracle stories and I prayed that one
day I'd be able to write a hopeful story on
one of those mammy forums!

Unfortunately, it wasn't to be. That night I
had terrible cramps in my tummy, like
awful period pain, and the spotting
reappeared. My mam suggested I rang the
early pregnancy ward at the hospital and
they told me to rest at home, take a
paracetamol and only be concerned if I was

soaking through pads. I took myself off to bed and tried to sleep. The following morning the bleeding had become a little stronger and the pains were increasing, so I spent most of that day getting in and out of the bath trying to get comfortable. At about 5pm the pains were unbearable, so I decided I'd try another bath. But within a few seconds of sitting down, the water started turning red. I felt dizzy. I had to call my parents as I didn't want to be alone, and, quite honestly, I was really scared.

They pulled up outside within minutes and then my dad drove me straight to the hospital. I was in agony by this time, and still bleeding heavily. I had been using hot water bottles to try and ease the pain, but nothing was helping.

By the time we got to hospital, I'd lost an awful lot of blood and I was rushed into see the consultant for a scan. He explained that I'd passed the baby but there was still a lot of blood in my uterus, and if I lost anymore I would have to be taken down for an emergency blood transfusion. I was given some pain relief, told to rest, and wheeled along to a side ward for the hospital staff to keep an eye on me.

The room was full of spiritual energy and for the first time ever, I felt as though my loved ones in spirit were coming through for me. Luckily, after a couple of days I was allowed to leave the hospital and go home, with strict instructions, again, to rest as much as possible. Matthew wasn't allowed home from Germany because the pregnancy was 12 weeks (so not classed technically as a 'viable' pregnancy) and I had to wait 3 days to see him.

Back home, and on my own for the first time after my miscarriage, I was lying in bed trying to watch a film. I kept drifting off to sleep and seeing white lights, mixed with streaks of gold which would then turn into a yellow tinge, as though it was the sun trying to peek through. I felt really warm, and tried to open my eyes again, but spirit wouldn't let me.

In my mind's eye I saw the most beautiful angel. She had long, flowing blonde hair, dainty features – almost like a pixie or a fairy, rather like Tinkerbell – and she whispered, "Shhh, she's sleeping."

At first, I didn't know what she was talking about. She had a book in her hand and was flicking through the pages. One page seemed to catch her eye and she stopped flicking, looked up at me and said,

"That's why we had to take her." On the page was a picture of my little girl – who I'd just lost. I stared at the page and underneath her picture were two dates: 13th December, 2011 – date of birth, and 23rd March, 2012, date of death, cause: 'Cot death'.

"That's why, Keely," the angel said. I knew at that point they were stopping me from going through the pain of losing a three-month old baby.

In front of her was a heavy, robed curtain and she told me to have a look. In the distance, I could see my gran in a rocking chair holding a tiny baby. The baby wore a beautiful pink cardigan, and my gran looked up at me and said,

"Come here quickly, do you want to hold her? You can have a quick hold."

I took hold of my baby in my arms and hugged her tight. I can still remember her special baby smell.

Far too quickly, Gran said, "You'll have to give her back now, Keely. Don't worry, she's safe here with me."

And then the whole vision faded and I could feel myself waking up again.

It was never confirmed by the hospital that I'd lost a baby girl but in my heart, I knew she was.

Chapter 6 ~ Chronic Illness

"Get up. Survive. Go back to bed."

In 2011, I had a miscarriage – this was to be my first of three – and after this, I began to feel really poorly. For months I couldn't shake off the feeling that I was getting 'flu. I was lethargic, and some days I couldn't even get out of bed. At times my heart would be beating so fast I thought it would jump out of my chest. My pulse would pound in my ears. I'd go dizzy and feel as though I were going to faint.

A couple of times I did actually black out, but managed to crawl back into bed and hoped that tomorrow was going to be a better day. Six months later, I'd had enough, and went to see the doctor. I described my symptoms and the doctor told me they were all related to anxiety. After all, I did have a lot to cope with (Matthew was in Iraq at this time). The doctor tested my bloods and the only thing that flagged up was my iron levels – they were on the low side. So I was put onto medication, and tried to get on with life.

Unfortunately, the tablets didn't make any difference at all, and in 2012, while my friend Kim was visiting, she had to call me an ambulance. I was getting really bad pains in my chest. I couldn't stand up because my heart was pounding so much. I thought I was having a heart attack.

The paramedics arrived and wired me to their machine. My heart was racing at 185 beats per minute - obviously, that isn't normal - so they took me to hospital and I underwent lots of tests. All of which came back normal, apart from my iron levels still showing as low. The consultant diagnosed my funny turn as an anxiety attack.

The next few months were a blur of doctor's appointments and I didn't feel right at all. Every time I stood up, I felt as though I was going to faint. Most of my days were spent in bed. My readings came to a standstill, and I just tried my hardest to pull myself together. But it was a real struggle. I can't describe how hard it was because I've always been active, I've always worked and been a go-getter. I felt as though I was in a trap I couldn't escape from.

One night, when I was feeling poorly, and helpless, I decided to Google my symptoms. I know you shouldn't do it but I was getting desperate at this point. Looking back, I'm so pleased I did my research. Every time I put in my symptoms the same thing kept cropping up – PoTS Syndrome, or Postural Orthostatic Tachycardia Syndrome, to give it its full title. The main symptoms were tiredness, rapid heart rate, brain fog, and a general unwell feeling. According to the NHS website it 'affects many different people, but is most common in girls and women aged 15 to 50.' I also read somewhere else that PoTS can be brought on after some kind of trauma to the body.

I searched for treatments in my local area, and came across a lady called Professor Julia Newton at Newcastle's RVI Hospital. I was desperate to speak to her and couldn't think of anything else. Should I contact her? Will she think I'm crazy? I decided against it and instead printed off everything I'd found about her, and this mysterious syndrome, and took it to my GP.

With PoTS, you can ask your GP for a poor man's test which involves your blood pressure and heart rate being taken whilst you're in a seated position and then again when you're stood up. If you have PoTS, your heart rate will skyrocket when you stand up and your blood pressure will drop considerably. At my highest, my heart rate was 188 beats a minute and my blood pressure dropped to 79/40 – it should be around 120/80 for my age.

When I went to see the GP, she sat me down and said, "Ok, you're going to tell me you have some rare form of cancer, aren't you?"

"No, but I think I have PoTS," I replied, and asked if she would do the poor man's test.

"Yes, ok, we can do the test."

She was surprised by the result, to say the least. "I'm just going to call in my junior doctor," she said.

And guess what? This junior doctor knew all about PoTS. Thank goodness for that! My GP sent off a referral to Professor Julia Newton at the RVI, and for the first time in a long time, I actually felt as though I was getting somewhere.

I had to wait months for this appointment to come through, so I began treating myself as though I had already got the PoTS diagnosis. I found out that to increase my blood pressure, I had to increase my salt intake. And I was drinking at least two litres of water a day to slow down my heart rate. Previously, I'd got into a bit of a caffeine rut and when I was tired I'd grab a cup of tea or a cappuccino, just like most people, so this took some getting used to. But I knew I had to do it. Eventually, my hospital appointment came through and I went to Newcastle to meet Julia.

I was wired up to an ECG monitor (which monitors your heart rate) and the nurse told me to lie down flat on the bed and keep still for ten minutes. Once this was complete, I had to stand up for ten minutes while they monitored my heart rate and blood pressure. I didn't quite manage to stand up for ten minutes, however, because during this time I nearly fainted. My heart rate had soared from 79 beats per minute when I was lying down to over 180 when I stood up.

When the consultant walked into the room, just five minutes after I'd stood up for the test, she told the nurse to turn off the ECG and asked me to sit down. She then went on to tell me that this was one of the worst cases of PoTS she had ever seen. I sobbed when she told me this – yes, it wasn't the best diagnosis, but after all these months and brick walls, I had finally got an answer.

She recommended I use Propranolol on the days when I couldn't get out of bed, that I increase my water intake to three litres a day, add salt to everything, and take one day at a time. I didn't just leave the hospital with a PoTS diagnosis that day either. The consultant also did a thorough search through my medical history and it emerged that I had been battling chronic fatigue and hypermobility.

She referred me to a pain management therapist at the RVI that day too – she clearly wasn't going to let me go away empty-handed! Vincent was the therapist, and he was wonderful. He's an absolute god and I still see him to this day. He talked everything through with me. At first he talked about getting into a routine, gave me tips to get out of bed on my groggy days, and talked about increasing my fluids and eating a healthy diet. I left the RVI that day so much more knowledgeable, and for the first time in about a year I felt like I could finally take on the world!

I didn't start on the medication because I knew I wanted to go down the alternative route instead. ***Disclaimer – please do not go against any professional medical advice you have been given, this was my personal choice.***

So when I got home, I fired up Google, and decided to begin my healing process by getting my chakras realigned. This took a couple of months in full – every three weeks I would go for reiki, and every one of my chakras healed beautifully, except my heart. My heart chakra was holding all the loss, and everything had congested there.

When I wasn't receiving reiki, I used a heart chakra healing meditation app on my phone. I would take two to three Epsom salt baths a week, and add some essential oils. ***Another disclaimer – before you start using essential oils please check with your doctor and/or an essential oil expert/specialist.***

My favourite essential oil is lavender because it relaxes me at bedtime and is a great way to lower my heart rate. The biggest thing for me on my healing journey was routine.

So I started off small by getting up at 8am every day, and making sure that I ate breakfast. I drank 500ml of water before I got out of bed to raise my blood pressure. My diet had a complete makeover, and I cut out wheat and gluten, and ate more fruit, vegetables and wholegrains. I started going out for walks – something I hadn't done for a long time – and enjoying the fresh air and the sunshine on my face. It was so good to feel alive again.

I also discovered a book called *The Secret* by Rhonda Byrne, and developed a whole new positive mindset based on the law of attraction.

I couldn't believe the change in me after just three months. These small and slight improvements were having a huge impact on the quality of my life.

During meditation one day, Greg came to me, and explained it was time to start my readings again. He said that Archangel Michael and Archangel Raphael were going to be beside me every step of the way, and that this was my path. I had to work with spirit. A couple of weeks later I took Greg's advice and began to see two to three clients a week. I desperately wanted to help people again, and build my business, and before I knew it, my diary was full for weeks in advance.

I absolutely loved it. Boom, boom, I'm back in the room was one of my favourite sayings at that time!

I should mention something else here. By this time, Matthew had left the army and having him at home all the time made things so much better. He helped me with my routine. He began working with my dad, and started at 8am, so our mornings started off perfectly. No more army life, no more chaos. We didn't have the worry or build up about where he was going next. No more feeling vulnerable as I laid in bed, alone, each night. It was our time now.

We could be a normal couple, go out for meals, to the cinema and do all the things normal couples do. It was just so nice to have my best buddy around again – permanently. All the laughs and giggles were certainly doing their job and my heart chakra was healing. Life was good. So good, in fact, we decided to try for another baby. Julia, my consultant, had reassured me I could still go on to have a baby, despite the PoTS diagnosis.

We were so excited when, in 2015, I found out I was pregnant again. We booked in for a private early scan when I was just six weeks pregnant. I can't tell you how relieved we were to see our healthy-looking little blob on the screen, and hear such a strong heartbeat.

Because of my miscarriage history, my consultant kept a closer eye on me, and I went to my local hospital two weeks later (at eight weeks pregnant) for my first 'official' scan. We were both excited for the scan again, and really thought everything was going to be fine. Sadly, it wasn't to be. We'd lost another baby. Obviously, once more, we were both heartbroken.

A few months later, I had an appointment with Julia at Newcastle and I mentioned my recurring miscarriages. In true Julia style she instantly referred me to a gynaecologist back at home. And, to cut a long story short, we discovered I had a bicornate uterus - basically, it's a heart-shaped uterus - and one side was in better working condition than the other. This meant my chances of having a successful, full-term pregnancy were much lower than average.

When I learnt this, it just felt weird, particularly because Greg had always told me (and I'd been told in various meditations) I was going to have a little boy. I have always been able to see him, from the colour of his eyes and his hair, to the clothes I would dress him in, I knew my little boy was waiting for me. So, surprisingly, I didn't get too disheartened.

And then in November 2015, I found out I was pregnant again. This time was different though. I didn't feel the normal excitement most women do when they see that blue line on their pregnancy test. I didn't do anything different. I cracked on with work, and life, and basically pretended that I wasn't even pregnant. After three losses, you do give up hope of a successful pregnancy, and I think in my heart of hearts I was scared to admit I was pregnant in case I jinxed everything.

On Christmas Eve, 2015, I went to the doctor's surgery and informed my GP of the positive pregnancy tests. Luckily, they had a spare slot for a scan that day; all I had to do was get to the hospital (which is only 5 minutes away). And guess what? I was further on than I thought.

I was actually nine weeks' pregnant (not five or six, as I'd thought) and best of all, there was a strong, fast heartbeat and my healthy little boy was doing well. Although I was buzzing, and so was Matthew, I still couldn't get my hopes up. But deep, deep down, I knew everything would be all right.

Weeks passed, but something kept niggling me. I didn't feel any different. With my previous pregnancies, I'd felt really sick, quite ill, in fact, but this time I just felt completely normal. So to reassure us, we decided to go to Babybond – a clinic where you can pay for a private ultrasound. We ended up going once a fortnight, and ran up a hefty bill, but in our eyes, it was worth every penny.

We had more good news, too. Even though pregnancy usually increases your blood pressure, my PoTS was fine. In fact, as is the case sometimes, my pregnancy had actually reversed the syndrome. Don't get me wrong, I can't say I don't have PoTS anymore. It hasn't gone entirely. I do still have good and bad days. But I don't have the tachycardia, or the fainting episodes, and the chronic fatigue has gone too. I've been very lucky.

Something else I want to mention here about PoTS. If you have been diagnosed with this syndrome, or if anyone you know and love has PoTS, then I wouldn't hesitate to recommend you join their community. I have made so many friends for life through

this community – we call ourselves the
Potsy Twinnies. You don't have to feel
isolated, and sometimes it's just good to
talk with people who know what you're
feeling and thinking. Here's a link to the
PoTS UK website: http://www.potsuk.org/
where you can find all kinds of valuable
information and support.

Chapter 7 ~ Famous Encounters and Impending Doom

"All you need is faith, trust and a little pixie dust."

~Tinkerbell

"Because you can speak to dead people, does that mean you can channel celebrities whenever you want to?"

I get asked this question all the time. And the answer is "no". Spirit always have to come to me, and it's been like that forever. That isn't to say that I haven't had a few famous encounters, though.

Michael Jackson

Michael Jackson and his songs have always followed me around since I was a little girl. When I was young, one of my earliest memories from our family holidays, was sticking my head out of the sunroof of the car as we drove through Devon with Michael Jackson's *Billie Jean* blasting. I loved it. And Billie Jean became my pet name in the family.

When I was about four years old, I started dancing lessons and it seemed that whenever I was dancing in shows or exams, they were always accompanied by a Michael Jackson song. I can remember being chosen to dance on stage to *Thriller*, and *Bad,* two of my favourites. But whenever I saw Michael on TV, or I heard his songs, I always felt that his life was really unhappy (even though I was only four years old at this time).

Greg reinforced my thoughts, and told me that that this iconic man's life had been awful. Despite making so many people around the world incredibly happy with his music and performances, he was hiding an awful sadness. His childhood had been almost non-existent, and in Greg's words, 'he had been treated like a dog'. Even at the age of four I could empathise with him so much and would fill up with tears when I listened to his songs.

Anyway, fast-forward 20 years or so. I hadn't listened to any of Michael Jackson's music for a while but a couple of days before his death, I kept seeing him. He looked so gaunt. I didn't know if this was because he was worn out with rehearsing for his 'This is It' 50-concert tour, or whether it was something more sinister. He'd been the focus of much global media hype during this time, anyway, so I convinced myself this was why he kept appearing in my thoughts.

Around this time, my cousin, Megan, and me decided to buy his album when we were out shopping one day. As soon as we got back to the car, we fired up the stereo and were dancing and singing.

"He hasn't got long," I said to her during a pause between songs.

"What do you mean?" Megan asked.

"I think he's going to die in the next couple of days or so."

"Oh, Keely you're crackers!"

A couple of hours later, we walked into my parents' house and the TV was on. Michael Jackson's death was headline news.

"You were right, Keely. Oh my god," Megan said, astounded.

I couldn't find the words to reply.

It really was so weird – yes, even though I work with spirit every day and I should never underestimate the messages they give me – I was still so shocked.

"At least he's in a better place, and he'll be free of all his pain and suffering now," I said.

As the media circus fired up, I knew instantly that he had been murdered, and that it was definitely something to do with his personal physician, Conrad Murray. Sure enough, two years later, he was convicted of voluntary manslaughter. If only they'd asked me first.

In 2014, 5 years after his death, the Michael Jackson signs started firing up again. I used to prefer to listen to the radio on my CD player at that time, rather than play CDs. One day, however, after a busy day of readings, I was pottering around and I heard this massive bang. I ran back into my psychic room, and *Billie Jean* was playing at full volume. I was completely freaked out!

I ran over to the CD player, and turned the volume off. The CD had started to play on its own. The room was freezing cold. I felt as though somebody, or something, was stood behind me. Don't get me wrong here, I've worked with spirit all my life, and I'm not afraid of poltergeist or demons (even though I've never dabbled in the dark side) but for the first time, I felt spooked. I kept looking behind me. There was no one else in the room. However, as I glanced over my left shoulder for the third time I saw a shadow with a strange face. It looked as though it was melting (imagine a record melting in a fire and that will give you an idea) and it was very pale and waxy.

At this point, all I knew was that this was a male with black curly hair. He had a white t-shirt with a black shirt over the top, and his hands were stretched out towards me (imagine a stereotypical picture of a zombie and you won't be far wrong). His hands were all rotten. His fingers looked long and lumpy. He started walking towards me and I really freaked out.

"Do you need help?" I blurted out. My gut instinct was telling me that he needed help to cross over from this world to the next.

"Thank you, thank you," came a reply in a very timid voice. Upon hearing his quiet, softly spoken voice, I stopped feeling so scared. Being the white witch that I am, I started burning some white sage and put some rock salt down in the room to absorb any negative energy. From experience, I know that sage helps spirits cross over, so if I encounter any who are lost or stuck between two worlds, I use this to help them travel to their next destination.

I told Matthew about it when he came in from work and he laughed (as he does). I couldn't stop telling people about it. I rang my sister Emily.

"What? Are you telling me you've just had Michael Jackson in your psychic room?"

"Yes!"

"I bet it's because I bought you that glove thing," she laughed. The glove thing she was referring to was a sparkling hand ornament kind of thing that reminded us both of Michael Jackson – which is why she bought it for me.

"No really, Emily. I'm serious. He's visited me."

"I wonder if he liked it!"

"What?"

"The glove, you loony!"

We had a bit of a giggle, and for the first time in a long time I actually thought I was starting to crack up. The spirits had finally broken me! It wasn't until a few days later, though, when I was mopping the kitchen floor, and something even spookier happened.

I could hear the rhythmic tapping of feet across the laminate flooring. I checked around to see where the dog was. She was in her kennel outside. Oh, yes, I am definitely cracking up, I thought.

I gave myself a good talking to, took a deep breath and got back to my mopping. Then I heard it again. The tapping was getting closer. I turned around and saw shoeprints on the wet floor behind me. This was getting too weird now. I poured some more bleach into my bucket and mopped over the footprints. They disappeared for a few seconds but then they came back. For anyone who thinks they were probably my footprints, let me just explain here that I have tiny feet – size 3 – so there's no way these prints were mine. Plus, I always mop my floor in bare feet – it's something I've always done. These footprints were man-sized. Matthew was out, the dog was in her kennel, and there was no one else around.

I tried to shake off the fear that was creeping up inside me, and turned back to my mopping. The rhythmic tapping started again. This time, and please excuse my French here, I shit myself, threw the mop down and ran upstairs.

My heart was pounding out of my chest, and I thought the best thing to do would be to just stay upstairs for a little bit and catch my breath. After a while I pulled myself together, gathered my thoughts and that was that. I went back to sort out the kitchen and everything seemed 'normal' again -whatever normal is for me.

A few nights later – this is the scary bit – Matthew was on nightshift and I was fast asleep. At 3.33 I was woken up by the bedroom door being pushed open with force. I heard the rhythmic tapping across the floor, again. Do you know that feeling when you're watching a scary movie and you just want to hide under the duvet and stay there forever? That was me.

Then I heard that voice again.

"Keely. Help me. It's Michael."

I could just make out his shadow as he sat on the end of my bed. He kept telling me that he was stuck, and that he needed me to show him the light. He needed to move on from this limbo existence.

For anyone who doesn't understand what I mean here, let me explain. I call the place between heaven and earth 'The Hall of Healing'. It's for people who have been really ill, whether mentally or physically. They sometimes get stuck there, and are unable to move on to where they're supposed to be, until their body and mind are physically rested. Sometimes this can take days, and at its worst, it can take years. I should also point out that if you go to see a medium and your loved one doesn't come through, it can be because this is where they are. They have not yet fully crossed over. Passing to the next realm is something which takes time, and until they've gone through the vortex to heaven, they won't be able to appear to loved ones on earth.

I've had many calls over the years from people wanting my help to move spirit from their house. 99% of the time, however, these energies aren't bad at all. They are simply stuck, and need help to cross over. Sometimes priests (armed with their holy water) do the same thing.

If you're reading this and you're wondering if you have a negative energy in your home, please be assured that it could just be a mischievous spirit. On the rare occasion that you're living in a house where a person was evil in this life, they can go on to be evil in the next, if they have not been shown the light correctly. A splash of holy water, and a little sage smudging, usually does the trick.

Back to Michael's story now. So he was sat on the end of my bed, asking for my help, and he stretched his hands out towards me again.

Then Greg appeared and said, "Ask him if you can put the bedside lamp on so you don't feel scared." So I did.

"Do whatever makes you feel happy, Keely. I'm sorry I look scary."

I put my hands out and Michael put his hands in mine. I said The Lord's Prayer over and over again. I don't know what possessed me to do that – my Catholic school years or the fact that I knew his family had been religious perhaps – but it just felt like the right thing to do.

We sat there for about 15 minutes – Michael's hands were freezing at first but then they began to warm up – and his energy flipped from dark and defensive to open and light. It was as if a massive cloud had been lifted. All I felt was this warmth radiating from him, and his melted face was starting to form again. Although his face still looked scary, his eyes were sparkling with happiness.

"Thank you, Keely. Thank you," he repeated, before he finally disappeared.

Once he was gone, Greg appeared. "Well that was an experience, wasn't it?" he said.

"Certainly was, Greg!" I replied, and wrapped myself up in the quilt to go back to sleep.

For days and days afterwards, I was completely shattered. When my energy levels picked up again, I did a full house cleanse. I opened the windows, changed my bedding, and literally cleaned every nook and cranny in the house. I just felt like I had to give everywhere a good declutter.

Every time I hear a Michael Jackson song now, I don't associate him with pain and suffering anymore. I know that he's happy now. He's warm, and he's loved and protected in the spirit world. He is finally free.

To this day, I've never had another visit from Michael, but I do think he'll return in the future at some point. He has appeared to me in dreams to show me that he's happy and he's partying. I think he likes to let me know he's ok every now and again.

Jade Goody

The passing of Jade Goody was completely different to Michael Jackson. There was a media build-up, and no one could escape the latest update on her tragic decline. For weeks before her death, I knew she was going to pass on Mother's Day. I kept seeing bunches of flowers and that's always my signal that it's a 'mother' association.

In the days before her passing I tried to send her distance reiki, and prayed regularly for a miracle for her – just like many other people did too. According to the media, Jade had a peaceful passing on 22nd March, 2009, surrounded by her loved ones. I believe she had been able to pass to the other realm a lot quicker than most people.

Two or three weeks later, I was doing a meditation – I like to meditate regularly, just to ground myself – and as I got deeper and deeper into the meditation, I went really warm. When I go warm, it's a sign that spirit is coming in close. I began to feel

nauseous and my eyes were flickering.
They felt like they wanted to open even
though I was in deep meditation and
always keep my eyes closed. I could hear
Greg telling me to open my eyes.

"You've got a special visitor," he said, "open
your eyes."

So I did. In a haze, right in front of me, I
saw this gorgeous girl, and she was
dancing to *YMCA*. All I could hear was this
infectious laugh, and her vision came
closer and closer to me, and when I looked
it was Jade. She looked totally different to
how she had appeared in recent
newspapers and magazines.

She had gorgeous, long, flowing hair, and
her trademark smile was beautiful, and
contagious. She looked as though she was
on a podium in some sort of nightclub, and
she kept saying to me,

"I'm enjoying the party. I'm enjoying the
party." Again, she started coming closer
and closer, and I could see her lips moving.
She was telling me all about heaven, and
how amazing it was, and that she wasn't in
any pain anymore. She was all better and

felt well again. Just like the old Jade. She started fading into the background, and the haze disappeared.

It was a heart-warming experience, and I felt so privileged that she had chosen to appear to me that day.

Since her passing, Jade has appeared to me about three times, and always during meditation. I always know it's her because of her giggle. On one occasion she told me that her son was going to become a doctor, and that her mum will find the right partner, and be very happy one day. The strongest message I always get from Jade, and which I want to reiterate here, is that she is absolutely fine now, and enjoying every last bit of heaven.

Celebrities Still on the Earth Plane

As a psychic, I get to hear lots of very personal and private information that many people wouldn't feel privy to sharing outside of their closest circles. So I've become something of an expert at keeping secrets. This comes in particularly handy when I meet celebrity clients.

I love reading for celebrity clients, as it's always very exciting. What usually happens is that I receive a phone call from the celebrity's manager, or management team who tell me they have a 'client' who is desperate for a reading. They tell me when they'll be in the north-east, and suggest a meeting place (usually a really nice hotel) and time.

When I get to the hotel, I still have no idea who I'm going to be reading for. Obviously, they don't want me to know, just in case I do a bit of research beforehand – which I would never do, but this covers both parties). I give the management rep's name to the receptionist/concierge, who then gives me a disclaimer/confidentiality agreement to sign. They then give me the payment for the reading, and I'm taken to a room.

The celebrity is usually sat there waiting for me, and, assuming I'm not too star-struck, I'll manage to break the ice quickly, and we'll get down to business. I do find it easy to build up a rapport with people, and this helps the reading flow. Sometimes I have to give my head a shake when I leave after reading for a particularly well-known celeb. I love my job!

Another good thing about reading for celebs is that I get to read about them in the media and see that some of the predictions I've made for them have come true. You don't always get this with local clients until many years later when they come back for another reading, and they fill in the blanks.

Impending Doom

Although, like I say, I love my job. There are times when it has its downsides, too. Let me explain. All of my life I have been able to feel when something really bad is going to happen. I get physical symptoms – I feel like I'm having a heart attack, my body aches, I get pains all over, and if I close my eyes, it's completely blackness.

The first time this happened to me was when I was 12 years old. It was a freezing cold November day, and all morning I'd felt really sick and unsettled. My mam had to force me to go to my weekly horse riding lesson, and the whole time that I was there, I just wanted to be back home.

It's funny what sticks in your mind but I remember feeling a bit scared by a bird that had got into the Equestrian Centre and was flying around. My teacher told me to concentrate on the horse and to canter. So as I gently kicked the horse, and started breaking into a canter, I heard Greg's voice.

"He's going to die."

"Who's going to die?" I replied.

"You know who," came Greg's answer.

So at that point, I started panicking. I thought the horse was going to die. I got a little wobbly and nearly fell off the horse. After a few seconds, I tried to push the thought to the back of my head and concentrate on my lesson.

When I got home that lunchtime, my dad pulled me to one side.

"Keely, your granddad's been taken into hospital. He's had a heart attack."

I was absolutely devastated. I sobbed and sobbed. I idolised my granddad. He was very poorly, apparently. So poorly that I wasn't allowed to go and see him. I'd only been with him the day before. We'd been getting conkers from the tree and he'd tied them onto black shoelaces for me. I kept those conkers and shoelaces for years afterwards. All afternoon, I kept crying and thinking about my granddad, willing him to get better.

But it wasn't to be. As me and my family sat watching *Heartbeat* on the TV, the phone rang.

My dad looked at me and said, "Go on, Keely."

"He's gone, Dad."

And I picked up the phone. My uncle was on the other end, "Put your dad on Keely." I passed the phone to my dad and he instantly burst into tears.

That's the day that my life changed forever. There isn't a day goes by when I don't think about Grandad Georgie Porgie Pudding and Pie Hopper.

*****

The second time I experienced this feeling of impending doom was back in 2001. I couldn't settle at all. I constantly felt on edge, as if something awful was going to happen. What was so bizarre that day was that it was so quiet at work, in the travel agents, so our manager let us take a break. My friend and me walked along the high street and passed a shop with lots of TVs in the window. My washing machine stomach fired up.

"Look, it's Independence Day," I said.

"That's not Independence Day. It's live. Something's happening," she replied.

Just as the words came out of her mouth, the second plane hit the twin towers, live on TV. The feeling of being on edge and not knowing why lifted instantly. We ran back to work and told everyone, and because we weren't allowed to have the radio on, and obviously no TV, we couldn't find out what was going on. Before long, however, the phones were ringing off their hooks, and we were swamped with requests to get our customers back from America as quickly and as safely as possible.

This is something that will always stay in mind, as it will for many other people, I'm sure. To me, it's the day the world changed forever.

*****

The last time I experienced impending doom was the night before my uncle passed away.

A few days earlier I'd had my tarot cards out, and shuffled them for myself, which is something I never do. My cards were awful. The death cards were there. I vowed that I would never use my tarot cards for myself ever again.

To this day, I don't know what possessed me to do them; a hunch, I guess, but it was as if I was supposed to receive a warning about something. Even Greg had questioned my decision to read for myself.

"It's not good, Keely. Why are you even looking at your tarot cards?"

At that point, I heard a rustle from the chimney and a pigeon dropped into my fireplace. It flew around the dining room. I screamed, and luckily Matthew was home, so he managed to get it out. Birds in the house, to me, is a sign of death.

On the day my uncle died, I couldn't settle at all. I couldn't get out of bed either, and I felt so ill I thought I was going to die. Even Matthew was worried. So worried, in fact, that he took some time off work because we didn't know what was wrong with me. When I was at work earlier that day, every time I closed my eyes I would see loose horses on the run, and I had no idea why. I soon found out, though, when my dad called later that night. My uncle had been killed on the bypass in Bishop Auckland.

He had been knocked off his horse and cart and died instantly. My cousin, who was only 12 years old at the time, had been knocked off his horse and trap as well, and was clinging onto life in intensive care. My uncle left behind my lovely aunty and my 5- year-old cousin, Megan. As soon as I received this news, the anxious feeling I'd been struggling with suddenly lifted. But obviously, that's when the mourning again.

Weeks later when I spoke to my aunty, she told me that a robin had found its way into her house the day my uncle died. It had flown around every single room in the house because all the doors were open. She also told me she remembered a massive blackbird tapping on her front door window the day my grandad died.

She also told me that my uncle's friend died a few weeks after him, in exactly the same way as he made his way to Appleby horse fair. When my aunty spoke to his mam, she told her that a big magpie had flown into her home too. It had flown up to his old, childhood bedroom, circled it and then flew out the way it came in. She got news a few hours later of his death.

*****

A couple of years prior to that, my parents were on holiday in Gran Canaria and due to return home. I'd been staying at a friend's house, and couldn't shake off this awful feeling. It wasn't because I was in a strange place, I'd stayed there lots of times before, and it wasn't because I was unhappy or homesick. I just didn't feel right.

Greg had said to me, "Your dad's not well. You need to ring your mam."

I tried to ring her a few times but there was no reply. Back in those days, mobile phones were just emerging, so apart from my landline, I had no other way of getting in touch. But I didn't think too much of it. I tried to get on with my day but this feeling was still lurking. I felt dizzy, sick and sweaty, and again, I couldn't put my finger on what was wrong.

When I eventually got hold of my mam, she and my dad had just touched down at Manchester airport. As always, my gut instinct had been correct. My dad had been poorly on the plane. He'd had a seizure, known as a vasovagal, due to a lack of oxygen to his brain. He'd said he wasn't feeling well and just as he got up to head towards the toilet, he slumped over and fainted. My mam was scared stiff and began running up and down the aircraft, shouting for a medic. They pulled my dad to the back of the plane and looked after him until he regained consciousness.

They weren't sure if he'd had a stroke at the time, because his whole body had gone weak. They sat him next to a doctor, and gave him a banana to eat to sort out his sugar levels. It was the scariest 2.5 hours of my mam's life. What I didn't know back at home was that I'd picked up on all his symptoms. He'd felt dizzy and sick and sweaty before the seizure.

That day changed my life, too, because since then I've only ever flown with him once. I don't feel comfortable flying with him anymore, and I worry myself sick when he boards a plane. Thankfully, their holidays abroad are a thing of the past now because they prefer touring the UK.

The only other time my dad had a similar episode was when he was working up in the sticks. He hadn't felt well all day and hadn't eaten much, either. He fainted again. Luckily, he was working with someone that day, and his workmate managed to get him pulled round, and give him something to eat. As he came round, a little robin redbreast appeared from nowhere and started tapping on the van window.

When my dad found out about this later, the first thing he said was, "Whatever you do, don't tell Keely." He knew I would freak out!

As well as the bird in my aunty's house on that awful day, and this robin redbreast, I've had another awful encounter with birds.

I used to look after Skye, my cousin's daughter (my god-daughter) two days a week, and one morning, when my cousin dropped her off she'd noticed a dead robin on the floor. Knowing that birds freak me out, particularly dead ones, she'd kicked it under the bush so I wouldn't see it. Then she'd gone off to work and thought no more about the dead robin... until she got a call later that day to say that her mam had been rushed into hospital. She'd collapsed at home, with a brain aneurism. Sadly, she died later that day.

*****

My god-daughter is like the daughter I've never had. I love her to pieces, and I know she is so loved by spirit too. I've taken photographs and videos of her dancing (she has the dancing bug just like me), and there have been orbs everywhere - all

captured perfectly on film and camera.
Skye comes out with all kinds of things
that let us know her nana is still around,
too, so at least we all get some comfort from
her unexpected and sad passing.

Before I finish this chapter, I just wanted to
point something out about my bird
experiences. Firstly, I don't like birds, and
secondly, I see them as a sign of impending
doom.

This is my personal take. So please don't
assume that this is right and how you feel
about birds is wrong. I know so many
people who find comfort in spotting a little
robin redbreast in their garden. And I do
know that spirit can return in this form
(and butterflies, too).

So as with everything spirit-related, take
what feels comfortable for you, and let the
rest go. As humans, we all have very
different experiences of life.

Chapter 8 ~ Proof That Readings Can Really Come True

"Sometimes when all your dreams may have seen better days. And you don't know how or why, but you've lost your way. Have no fear when your tears are fallin'. I will hear your spirit callin'. And I swear I'll be there come what may."

~ Hanson

I've been privileged to give readings to hundreds of people throughout my life (probably into the thousands if I'm honest) and I always love to hear from people whose predictions have come true.

At times, I may have to wait months or years for an update, which is absolutely fine – spirit will not be rushed! But there have been times when I have literally only had to wait a few hours for the proof to arrive. I love the quick ones the best!

To give you a sample of the kind of proof I've received that readings can, and do, come true, here is a snippet of stories which do just that.

Happy Ever After

One day, a young girl come for a reading. She told me she felt like she was terrible at relationships, and that she felt like giving up all hope of ever finding a partner. I looked through her cards and told her not to worry, and that her heart would be eventually healed. There was, in fact, a wonderful man on his way to her. I could see the disbelief on her face.

"In fact," I said, "I'm seeing Iceland really clearly here. I can see flashing lights in the sky and stars." She looked at me as though I'd just fallen from a different planet. "I can see diamonds and sparkles, and on 25th December this will all make sense to you."

A few years later, this lovely girl got in touch. After her reading she'd written everything down and she'd kept this piece of paper. The year after her reading, she met the love of her life who had taken her to Iceland for Christmas Day and proposed under the northern lights, with a big, shiny diamond ring. And they really did live happily ever after.

Happy Ever After Part 2

Another lovely lady came to me a couple of times for readings. On both occasions, I kept seeing a beautiful little blue-eyed girl in her cards.

Whenever I mentioned this, she would say, "No, I'll never have a little girl. They don't run in my family. We only have boys." But I was adamant that she would have this gorgeous little girl.

She said, "I hope you're right because if I get pregnant again, I really don't want another little boy." She had two already. A few months later she got in touch to tell me she was pregnant. Again, I reassured her that she was definitely having a girl.

"I'm not sure. I feel the same as I did when I was carrying my boys."

About a year ago, I got sent a beautiful picture of this gorgeous baby girl. She had the same big blue eyes, and dark hair that I'd seen previously, and this lady was absolutely ecstatic that my prediction had come true.

She got her happy ever after, too.

A Reading Emergency

A gentleman came for a reading, and as he sat down in front of me, I remember feeling a crushing sensation on my chest. Greg had popped in, and he very clearly told me this man needed to go to hospital. There was something wrong with his heart. I asked him if he'd been experiencing a crushing sensation on his chest, and he told me he had, and that he hadn't mentioned it to anyone else.

"If you don't take anything else away from this reading, please just promise me that you'll go and get this checked out at the doctor's."

A couple of weeks later, this gentleman's wife got in touch to tell me he'd just come out of surgery. He'd had a triple heart bypass and if he hadn't come to see me that day, and took my warning seriously, the doctors had given him very little chance of survival.

Thankfully, he's now gone on to make a full recovery and is doing really well. His wife keeps me up to date about his health, and it's wonderful to know I played a part in helping him.

Sometimes it's not all about the good stuff, unfortunately.

One day, a beautiful young girl came through my door. I looked at her, and despite her beauty, I could through it. Spirit showed me lots of bruising around her body and face. As I shuffled her cards and she picked seven out, my stomach lurched. Her cards were awful. In fact, they were probably the worst cards I've ever seen someone pull out.

Greg popped in again, and said to me, "He's taken all of her money. She's pregnant, and she's starving. You can't charge her for this reading."

So before I started on her reading, I stood up and said, "Right before we go any further I'm going to put the kettle on and make you a sandwich."

She looked a little shocked but relieved at the same time.

"Do you need help?" I asked her.

"No, I'm ok."

"Well, listen I'm not going to charge you for this reading, as long as you do something for me. You must get away from that man. If you don't, I can see you getting badly hurt, and it won't be good for your unborn baby. The next time you go to the hospital for your midwife appointment, you need to explain what's going on and they'll be able to help you."

"No, I can't. He comes everywhere with me. I won't be able to talk to them on my own."

"Right, okay. Well, try something else instead. Go to the loo, and there'll be a poster on the back of the door with a number you can ring."

"What if he takes my phone off me?"

"Well you'll have to pull the emergency cord in the toilet, and someone will come in and help you."

This entire conversation was in whispers because her boyfriend was outside waiting for her in the car, and his sister – ie her chaperone, because she wasn't allowed anywhere on her own – was sat in my living room waiting for her reading. I found out that this awful man had turned the girl's family against her, and that she had absolutely nobody in her life except him (and his equally evil sister).

She ended up doing everything I'd advised her too, and she came back to see me a couple of months later. Her 'boyfriend' had been arrested and was going to court. He was later found guilty of attempted murder.

Now, thankfully, she's doing really well. She was moved to a refuge somewhere down the country, and her and baby are doing fine. I get regular updates from her, and, again, I'm so pleased and relieved that I was able to help her that day she came for a reading with me.

Chapter 9 ~ The Day-to-Day Reality of Working with Spirit

"Do more of what makes you happy."

~ Keely Potts

As I've mentioned lots of times in this book, I absolutely love my job. But, as any clairvoyant knows, there is no escaping it. That's why I've devoted this chapter to showing you what the day-to-day reality of working with spirit actually looks like – warts and all.

Many people are fascinated with the whole concept of spirit and being able to communicate with them. That probably explains why I get asked lots of questions when people find out what I do. Something I'm regularly asked, usually goes along the lines of… "Are you picking anything up for me right now, Keely?".

And just like the previous question I talked about at the start of this book ("Can you just tune into people, Keely?") the answer is still the same: no. I have to allow spirit to come to me. Very often, however, their timing isn't that great, and what's good for them, isn't necessarily good for me. Let me explain…

I was standing at the till in my local supermarket recently, loading up the conveyor belt with my shopping, and I reached for a bar of chocolate from a stand nearby. Coincidentally, the woman who was standing in front of me also reached for the same bar of chocolate. As her hand touched mine, and we smiled at each other awkwardly, I immediately felt the presence of her daughter in spirit. I heard a voice whisper in my ear, "Tell her Kimberly is here with her. Tell her it's Monday, our shopping day."

Oh, dear, I thought. Someone else is going to think I'm a complete nutter. But hey ho, in for a penny, in for a pound.

"Excuse me, I hope you don't mind but I'm a clairvoyant and I've just been given a message to pass on to you. Is that ok?"

"Erm, yes," said the woman, surprised.

I passed on the message and after the initial shock, this lady was over the moon with her message. She did, indeed, have a daughter in spirit, called Kimberly, and they always used to do their shopping together on a Monday.

*****

Another time, I was Christmas shopping with Matthew and searching for an outfit. There was a guy on the till who looked, shall we say, slightly rough around the edges – full of piercings and tattoos – and definitely not your stereotypical high-street shop kind of salesperson.

Anyway, I was stood in the queue and my washing machine tummy fired up. I went all hot and sweaty, and I knew spirit were close. Greg appeared behind me and whispered in my ear.

"His mate was in a car accident," he said and pointed at the shop worker. "Tell him he loves his new tattoo that he's had done in his memory."

I got to the front of the queue and my heart was pounding. I knew I had to pass this message on but it wasn't exactly the most convenient place to do so. I started getting twitchy, which is Matthew's cue to leave.

"I'll just be out here," he said as he walked out the shop. Typical Matthew.

Left to my own devices, I couldn't hold back and before I could even think about it the words blurted out of my mouth.

"Your friend who died in the car accident loves your new tattoo." I then went on to describe the tattoo to him, which was on his leg, and this big, butch, biker-looking guy lifted up his trouser leg and showed me just what I'd described. He looked as though he was going to faint.

"How the flamin' hell did you know that?"

"I'm a clairvoyant and I sometimes have no control over what spirit want me to share with people."

He then burst into tears and I realised just how important it was for him to hear this message.

Being psychic, or clairvoyant, or a medium – however you want to describe it - does sometimes mean I have little control over the things that happen, but I wouldn't change it for the world.

It can get exhausting sometimes, too, though, because you can't escape spirit. Even when you're on holiday and supposed to be recharging your batteries, spirit seem to enjoy just popping in and out at their will.

I remember a few years ago, Matthew and me decided to recharge in Malta. Basking on our loungers near the pool, one day, we were totally chilled, and enjoying the sunshine, when all of a sudden who should turn up? Yes, Greg. He came to Malta with us.

"You need to go over there, and tell that lady Monique is with her. She needs to hear it. Keely, she needs to hear it."

I remember actually blurting out loud. "For God's sake, Greg, they're not even English! How am I going to start this conversation?"

"You'll think of something. You always do."

I stood up, threw on my flipflops and stomped across the side of the swimming pool. To say I was feeling pretty annoyed that my sunbathing had been taken over by spirit yet again, was an understatement.

There were three women sat together, and the one Greg wanted me to speak to was quite haggard-looking, weathered shall we say.

"Excuse me, do you speak English?" I asked her.

"Only a little," she replied.

So I tried to explain that I picked up on spirit and energies, when out of my mouth popped the words, "Monique is on holiday with you."

The lady burst into tears. The two ladies who were with her – I later found out they were her sisters – were also in floods of tears.

"That's our mother," she said in broken English. "And this is our first holiday without her."

Greg said, "Tell her that she loves the crucifixes." So I did, and the lady sobbed even harder.

"Thank you, thank you so much," she managed to say and pointed to the ankle bracelet she was wearing. She then pointed to her sisters and I saw that each of them were wearing matching ankle bracelets, all with crucifixes on in their mother's memory. I later found out they had placed a crucifix on their mother's ankle too, in the chapel of rest.

During the rest of the holiday, our paths would cross almost every day, and each time they saw me, they would give me a hug, kiss my cheeks and call me "Angel Lady."

***

When we made another attempt at rest and relaxation, this time at the beautiful city of York, spirit, again, had other plans. We were staying in a hotel called 'The Jorvik' and all night I couldn't settle. Spirit were really hounding me! Greg told me to 'wake up and listen to what they were saying'. So I did.

This one male spirit was sat in the corner of the room sobbing. He told me he had hung himself from the ceiling beam. It was so sad. On the train ride home, my curiosity got the better of me and I Googled the hotel and its history. Lo and behold, I found out there had been a man who lived in the hotel in the 1800, and he had hung himself from the beam after hurting his wife and child, and guilt got the better of him.

A year later I went back to that hotel, and requested the same room. I took my sage incense, cleansed the entire room and crossed him over to the light. I haven't been back since but I really must pay that place a visit sometime again soon.

Charlie – Our Resident Ghost

Yes, we have a spirit (or ghost, if you prefer that label) in our house. He's called Charlie, and he's about 56 years old and he's an undertaker. And he loves nothing more than scaring the bejeepers out of everyone and anyone he can. He wears Victorian clothes, carries a walking cane, and he's tall and skinny. He looks a little like the Kiddy Catcher off *Chitty Chitty Bang Bang* but he's nowhere near as sinister.

He doesn't mean any harm to us, but he refuses to leave our home. If truth be known, I think he's a lonely man. He's told me he likes living with us, that he's happy here and he's staying here forever. He loves being a bit of a tinker, and his quirky sense of humour sometimes spooks me too.

For example, we might be watching a film when all of a sudden we hear *thud, thud, thud.* It takes a few seconds to realise what it is but then we remember it's Charlie. He's in his favourite place - on the stair landing - and he's tapping his cane on the bannister.

Charlie used to have a maid as well, called Elizabeth, and I have seen her in our house on a few occasions. She always emerges from the wall – like a proper ghost – and just seems to pop in and out when she feels like it. She'll sometimes nip in and say, "That lightbulb needs changing." And I know for a fact it's just been changed, but then I'll go to turn on the light and it will pop. That does get annoying sometimes.

Unfortunately, not everyone feels comfortable around our Charlie and

Elizabeth. We've even had builders working on the house who have refused to come back and finish the job. They might last a day or two, then things would start to happen. Their tools might go missing, and then they'd argue amongst themselves as to who'd last had it or who'd lost it, and then a couple of hours later, the tools would magically reappear.

Another time, we had some builders in to damp-proof our cellar and while they were busy working away, a chunk of stone was thrown across the room at them. All I heard was their footsteps running up the cellar stairs.

"That's it... sorry, Keely, but I'm not coming back!"

Luckily, my dad finished off the work.

Car keys disappear constantly in our house, and funnily enough, just as I'm writing this, I have no idea where my car key is. I've had to use the spare today. I know that by tonight it will have reappeared – usually on the armchair of the sofa – because that's what Charlie likes to do.

Being in contact with spirit can also be costly...

It's October 2017 now, and in this year alone I've gone through four vacuum cleaners. Believe it or not, this is a good year. I've gone through as many as seven vacuum cleaners in a year before. So I always, always, always take out a warranty!

If you're wondering what the connection is between things blowing up, popping, and malfunctioning, it's because spirit like to use electrical sources to make their presence known. It's their way of showing us that they're around. So if your lightbulbs need replacing every week or every month, then maybe it's not actually down to you buying cheap lightbulbs!

I have had my electrics checked time and time again, so I know there isn't a fault with our system. And every time we move house I get the electrics checked. I know deep down that this is spirit's way of playing with me, but I still err on the safe side, and always get my electrics checked out by a professional to put my mind at rest.

We've gone through four lightbulbs just this week – even the ones which say they'll last a lifetime. We've gone through three lawnmowers in one year, bearing in mind you only use it for half of the year, as well, that's a lot of lawn mowers.

The kettle is always switching itself on and off, and the radio and television switch themselves on whenever they feel like it. My toaster blew up the other day. The lights in our house are always flickering. We regularly have smells appearing – sometimes it's lavender (which I always put down to Elizabeth being around) and I've smelt baking bread in the house before (I don't have time to bake my own bread).

It's not just electrics and smells either. The other day, I started to run a bath for the baby and left the room to grab a clean towel. During the short time this took, the tap had gone from a tepid trickle to a full-on blast of cold water. I also went through a phase of having my locks changed regularly because they would always stick, and I would end up being locked in or locked out of my own house. The barrels in my external doors have been changed so many times we've lost count. The locksmith who came out to change them couldn't come up with a logical explanation as to why this kept happening.

My Secret Weapon - Sage

As strange as it sounds, I saged the doors, and so far, so good. Sage is burned to lift any negative energies or any nuisance spirits who shouldn't be there. You can buy sage in bundles or you can buy it in incense sticks and cones. It has a lovely, clean and fresh, woody kind of smell, and in witchcraft, sage is hung in bundles above the front door of a house to bring in good luck and keep the negative energies away.

I don't know if you've ever seen a traditional wreath before but if you have, you might have noticed it usually has sage on it (this is to repel negative energies, too) as well as holly for luck, cinnamon for wealth, and mistletoe for love.

Another thing you might find interesting about how spirit make their presence known, is that every time they come near me, my hands become really warm. If I sense that if someone is ill or if they have a broken heart, my hands will literally start to vibrate or shake. I'm sure that Graham and Liliana gave me the gift of healing that time when they helped me after I'd fallen at Mama Rosa and banged my head.

That's just a little snapshot of what it's like to live day to day with spirit energy flying around. And like I say, I love my job, but it isn't for the faint-hearted!

Chapter 10 ~ Tramadol Nights

"Head down, heels in."

~ Dad

As I've mentioned throughout this book, despite all the evidence I've been able to share with my family, my dad has never been much of a believer. He has always replied to anything I've told him about spirit with a logical explanation, or come up with an alternative reason for something happening. For most of my life he has had the most vivid dreams, and he has seen spirit (including loved ones who have passed over) and most recently Sir Bruce Forsyth, which even he thought was quite bizarre.

My dad is a strong character, rough and ready is the only way I can describe him. No one in their right mind would want to mess with him. I remember the children at primary school asking if he was one of The Mob because of his expensive cars. Because of his assertive and feisty personality, he has always been reluctant to accept that there is a spirit world, but there was a time in his life when they forced him to believe.

It was the winter of 2013, he and my mam had gone ski-ing to Italy. He fell over on the slopes – probably ski-ing far too fast, as usual – and bashed his shoulder. After that, he couldn't move it and was in a lot of pain, which was spreading into his chest. X-rays showed he hadn't broken any bones but after months of pain he was finally diagnosed with frozen shoulder. He had to have an operation where his shoulder was removed from its socket, some bone was shaved off, and then it was slotted back in again.

My dad has always been a hard worker, always busy, and he's always had a physical job, so as you can imagine, he struggled to rest after his op. Resting just doesn't feature on his radar – especially not for six weeks! He's never been a daytime TV kind of fella and still doesn't even know who Jeremy Kyle is.

But, on doctor's orders, he had to have complete bed rest for six weeks. He slowly drove my mam and me round the bend. The doctor had prescribed Tramadol for his pain, and if you've ever been on Tramadol, you might know the side-effects all too well. In my dad's case he was – in his words – tripping out his box.

One night, as he laid in bed and started to drift off to sleep, he saw four beautiful African women with bright red lips, standing at the foot of the bed. They were each taking turns to step forward and kiss him on the lips. To this day, he doesn't know if he was awake or asleep, but if truth be known, I think he quite enjoyed what was going on. That was until the door opened, and a little boy wearing a brown cap and knickerbockers peeped round and the women vanished.

"Hello, mister," said the little boy with a big smile which showed a missing tooth at the side of his mouth.

"Are you Greg?" replied my dad.

"Yes, mister. I'm Greg."

"Well you can get lost. I've had enough of you. You've caused my daughter so much trouble over the years. Just go away and leave us alone."

"What have I ever done to you, mister?"

"Just get out, Greg, just fuck off and don't come back!"

With that, Greg burst into tears, took off his cap, scratched his head and walked away. The next day, I'd gone to visit Dad and check up on him.

"I know I've never asked you this before, but can you tell me what Greg actually looks like?" he asked.

"Yes, he's about 12 years old, brown hair, brown cap, freckles, scruffy boots... oh, and Dad, he's got a tooth missing but it's not one of his front teeth, it's on the right-hand side."

My dad's face went eerily white.

"I think I'm going to be sick, Keely. I've got something to tell you. Greg was here last night and I told him to get lost."

"What do you mean, you told him to get lost?" I shouted.

"I told him I was sick of the trouble he'd caused you. But, Keely, I'm really sorry. I saw Greg and I know he's real now, and I'm sorry for never believing you all these years."

Greg had obviously taken offence at my dad's outburst, because for the first time in my life, he wasn't around. I didn't see him for four months and this had a huge impact on me and my work with spirit.

You see, when I do my readings, Greg is always with me. He tells me things that the cards don't because he's the bridge between heaven and earth, and passes on messages from loved ones in spirit.

So without him, I could only rely on my cards and I felt like I'd had my arm chopped off. Life without Greg was something I wasn't used to at all. I missed him so much, and I prayed every night for him to come back to me.

I was struggling personally, too, as during this time I'd lost a baby. This was my third miscarriage, and I felt completely and utterly alone. Obviously, my husband and family were a great support at this time, but things just weren't the same without Greg. He'd always been my little buddy.

Then one day, I was hanging out a bedsheet on the washing line and went to get a peg out the basket and who should appear?

"Hello, you." Greg said.

"You're back. Where have you been?" I couldn't believe he was actually back.

"Well your dad told me to go away. But I think I've been gone too long and I know you need me now."

And from that point, everything started to get back on track. My work began to take off. I was busy with bookings for readings, again, and people from all over the world were connecting with me. I'd gone from 5,000 likes on my Facebook page to 30,000 in the space of a few months without even trying. Spirit messages were getting stronger and stronger. My communication channels flowed much more easily with Greg around.

"Boom, boom, boom, I'm back in the room," as Greg would say.

Greg sauntered back into my life in his usual demure style. We were together again and about to take on the world.

Within half an hour of Greg's return, we jumped in my car, switched on *Mmmbop* by Hanson and cranked up the volume all the way to my parents' house. Dad had just got in from work.

"Dad, guess who's back? Guess who's in the car?"

"Please tell me it's Greg."

"He's back, Dad, he's back!"

"Thank God for that. Stick the kettle on." We got our cups of tea and made a little toast to Greg.

"You can't get rid of me that easily," I heard him say as he sat on the couch next to me.

Thank goodness for that, Greg!

Conclusion

So, there you have it, a little snapshot of my life, my spirit adventures and, of course, my infamous spirit guide, Greg. I hope you've enjoyed reading this book, and that it's sparked some interest for you in all things spirit.

If you could leave me a review on the Amazon Store, I'd be so grateful.

I'm sure there will be plenty of new books in the pipeline, because as the years go by and my experiences grow, I'll have more and more stories to share with you.

Until then, take care, and here's to our paths crossing again.

Connect with Keely

I'd love to connect with you, so please do come and find me on Facebook (that's my favourite place to hang out – and with Greg sometimes shows up too):

https://www.facebook.com/KeelyPotts-PsychicMedium-340663855955221/

You can use my Facebook page to keep up to date with all things Keely, you're your own private readings, and get some positive spiritual vibes going on!

About Keely

Keely Potts is an ordinary girl, as well as being a psychic medium.

She lives in Bishop Auckland, Co Durham, with her husband Matthew, her baby boy, Loxley, Indi, her dog, and of course, Greg, Charlie and Elizabeth (and probably a few more spirits who haven't been named yet)!

Keely loves her job as a clairvoyant, even though it sometimes puts her in the most awkward of positions, but she wouldn't change it for the world.

Oh, and she has big, big dreams for helping as many people around the world as she possibly can.

Printed in Poland
by Amazon Fulfillment
Poland Sp. z o.o., Wrocław